A Life in Pictures

DAVID JASON

A Life in Pictures

STAFFORD HILDRED
& TIM EWBANK

BLAKE

Published by Blake Publishing Ltd
3 Bramber Court, 2 Bramber Road
London W14 9PB

First published in hardback in Great Britain in 1999

ISBN 1 85782 301 X

British Library Cataloguing-in-Production Data:
A catalogue record for this book is available from the British Library.

Typeset by GDAdesign

Printed and bound in Great Britain by The Bath Press

Pictures reproduced by kind permission of People in Pictures, Alpha,
Rex Features, UPP, All Action, Pearson TV, Channel 4, BFI,
The Hornsey Journal, LWT and PA News.

Every effort has been made to contact the copyright holders,
but some were untraceable. We would be grateful if the relevant
owners would contact us.

Introduction

Introduction Introduction
Introduction

'This time next year we'll be millionaires,' was the popular motto of Del Boy and Rodney Trotter. They finally did make their fortune in the hilarious top-rated farewell three-parter of Britain's best-loved comedy show screened over Christmas 1996. In the junk of their lock-up garage Del's father-in-law found the missing John Harrison watch, which went on to sell for auction at Sotheby's for £6.2million.

Del was so astonished he fainted. But in real life the sum was rather less overwhelming for David Jason. His current personal fortune is now around twice that figure. After two decades of scintillating success in the increasingly competitive world of television, the name of David Jason is now firmly linked in the public perception with quality programmes and enormous audiences.

His remarkable comic timing, his mesmerising common touch as a master communicator, and his unerring eye at selecting only the exceptional scripts from the hundreds sent his way all add up to an almost priceless commodity.

A senior television executive confided: 'There are a select few TV actors at the very summit of their profession who can be guaranteed to deliver huge audiences, so long as the project is sound. John Thaw and Robson Green, certainly. Nigel Havers, Warren Clarke, Keith Allen, Nick Berry and Kevin Whately sometimes. Ross Kemp very probably. But if I had to put my shirt on making a new series and I needed a real star to carry it through to the public I would go for David Jason every time. He has that indefinable X factor. People know him and they trust him and they like him. He could read out the London telephone directory and get an audience.'

That popularity has a large price, but it is not primarily financial. David has a long established understanding with Yorkshire Television that is based more on mutual respect and trust that the high production standards will be maintained than money. Nevertheless the son of a Billingsgate fish porter refuses to sell himself short. So Yorkshire are more than happy to pay £1.3 million per year to their favourite star for a wonderful non-exclusive contract to make quality dramas like *A Touch of Frost* and John Sullivan's planned *Micawber* series as well as his beloved daredevil scuba-diving programmes, but David is still left free to pick and choose pet projects from elsewhere.

The BBC paid David £250,000 to play real-life hero Captain Frank Beck in their momentous war film *All The King's Men* in autumn 1999. He is still much in demand for voice-over work for animations and adverts but he is much more selective these days.

The popularity of David's work constantly swells his bank balance. Although early *Only Fools and Horses* contracts were by no means lucrative, the 50% repeat fees are regularly clocking up all the time. And for each of the farewell trilogies David was paid a BBC comedy record of £69,000.

What is not so well known is that David Jason regularly makes large anonymous donations to charities, often cancer charities in memory of his long-term companion Myfanwy Talog. And he frequently helps out people less well off than himself. One actor who asked to remain anonymous was hit by a crippling asthma attack which lost him work and was in danger of losing him his house until David heard about his plight and quietly sent round a large cheque to tide him over.

David Jason is now worth around £12.5million but at his current rate he will almost certainly never spend it all. He enjoys exotic holidays and has a large country house and a Jaguar, but he hates wasting money and is appalled by stars who flaunt their wealth. His relationship with Yorkshire TV boss David Reynolds is at the heart of his biggest contract and when he first went to Reynolds' house to discuss his future, David Jason spent more time unblocking a drain than he did demanding money. He prefers to negotiate a good deal and conditions for the team that surrounds him than to try to drive the hardest of bargains.

Now, more than ever, David declines to talk about his wealth. 'I was brought up to respect money and I am not going to change,' he says. But long after he has earned more money than he will ever spend, he continues to work hard and bring enjoyment to millions. 'I'm just delighted to be doing a job I love,' says David.

The money has been well earned, though, and the path to the amazing success he now enjoys has been a hard-fought one…

Opposite page:
The nation's favourite faces.

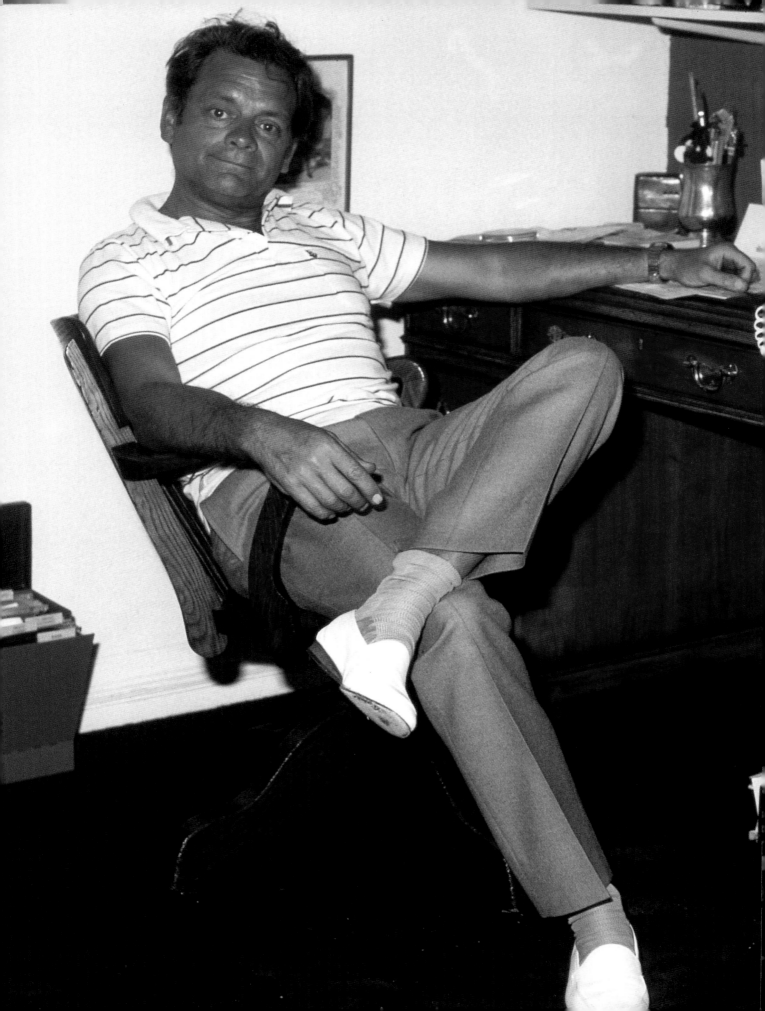

CHAPTER ONE

Childhood

Childhood
Childhood

David Jason richly deserves his reputation as Britain's most popular comedy actor and today many millions of people enjoy his hilarious antics on television, particularly as Derek Trotter in his greatest success the BBC's Only Fools and Horses. *But as he grew up in post-War London the young David was every bit as funny without a script, as one hapless Finchley window cleaner could testify.*

David was brought up in a tiny terraced house, 26 Lodge Lane, which has long since been demolished to provide land for a car park. A regular visitor to the sleepy suburbs in those days was a window cleaner with an unhappy reputation for being something of a dirty old man. Horse drawn carts were still a familiar feature of the North London traffic then, and the window cleaner always carried buckets to scoop up the horse droppings to sell as manure to rose growers. This meant his barrow was usually laden with buckets of steaming natural fertiliser as well as ladders.

To brighten one dull summer day David thoughtfully inserted two bangers deep into one bucket, lit the fuse and made a run for it. The resulting explosion left the poor window cleaner and a couple of innocent passers-by covered from head to toe in horse muck. Childhood friend Julie Pressland remembers the incident clearly.

He just loved to make people laugh.

'We all thought the window cleaner was a pervert so no-one was very sorry for him,' she says. 'It was a real mess. There was horse muck everywhere. The window cleaner was really mad.

'That was pretty typical of David. He was full of devilment but he never did anyone any real harm. It was just for a joke. He just loved to make people laugh. He had an air gun and he filled another neighbour's tin bath full of holes. We had some washing strung out on a line in the back yard and my mum kept looking out and saying, "There's a funny wind—it's only blowing the knickers." David was hanging out of his back window taking pot shots at our underwear with his toy gun! There were five women in our family so there were always plenty of drawers on the line for him to aim at.'

David was born on 2 February 1940, as World War II raged bitterly across Europe, in the middle of one of the coldest winters in years. His father,

David's birth certificate.

Billingsgate fish porter Arthur White, and his mother Olwen, already had a seven-year-old son also called Arthur. And David had a twin brother who sadly died at two weeks. 'I was in such despair,' said Olwen bleakly, years later. 'We had decided to call the twins David and Jason. David was healthy but Jason was so sickly he never had a chance and I felt so helpless.'

But the healthy twin thrived and David John White was a lively baby with a powerful set of lungs which he was always eager to demonstrate for his grieving parents. Olwen was naturally especially delighted when her surviving twin eventually went on to make the two names so well loved and famous throughout the land. Yet it was not until David was 14 that he discovered he was a twin and that his baby brother had died. He told the authors: 'It just came out during the course of some conversation with my mother that apparently I had had a twin.'

Baby David did his bit for the family war effort by noisily resisting attempts to put on his tiny gas mask. Whenever the air raid sirens sounded and the family started to move to the relative safety of the shelter erected in the house, David's screams of protest began. 'It used to worry me a lot, that gas mask,' recalls Olwen. 'He just screamed like mad when I put it on him.'

Often David's cries had to compete against the noise of German air raids which used to inspire his mother to retaliate by hurling curses in the direction of Berlin as she crashed dishes around in her anger in her tiny kitchen. Once the Luftwaffe almost silenced these fierce reactions with a near miss of a bomb which left the house structurally undamaged but somehow managed to blow out Olwen's cooker. Happily the only casualty was the cake she was baking at the time.

Olwen was determined to protect her brood from the worst of the War. She brought her brisk efficiency and warm sense of humour from her native Wales. A baby girl, June, completed the family four years after David was born. And while there was never much money to go around the fiercely independent Olwen supplemented her husband's meagre wages by going out and working as a cleaner.

David's brother Arthur was always a boisterous lad and came close to ending one of Britain's most promising acting careers some 20 years before it began, with a badly aimed housebrick. Arthur said: 'David wanted to come to a camp I had made with my mates. I wouldn't let him, and he was hanging about trying to get in. Unfortunately, he got in the way of a brick I was throwing at our "enemies". It hit him on the head and nearly killed him. I was shattered and to this day he still carries the scar.'

Baby David did his bit for the family war effort by noisily resisting attempts to put on his tiny gas mask.

It was certainly obvious to all the family that David's flair for acting was there from a very early age. Olwen found her children's favourite game was dressing up. Her frilly blouses and floppy hats, dresses and coats and her husband's trousers and shirts were all in constant demand from the three youngsters who loved to act out their own little plays. Arthur, the oldest, generally took the early lead in the junior White dramatic society but David and June always seemed to be playing the biggest parts by the end.

When they got older they pestered their mother to take them to scour junk shops for even more outlandish outfits. Olwen encouraged the artistic side in her offspring. She was steeped in the Welsh family tradition of creating your own entertainment with large gatherings with every relation called upon to deliver a song or a monologue.

David is shown here, far left, in his early days with his amateur drama group the Incognitos.

When the children moved on to nearby Northside School it was June who impressed dramatically with a spirited portrayal of Queen Victoria in an early school play. David's cheeky sense of humour certainly began to develop. His best friend was a lad called Mike Weedon who lived just two streets away in Grange Avenue. The two youngsters made sure that life was never dull for their English teacher, an endlessly harassed lady called Miss Holmes. Mike recalls that one of David's early pranks was to spray on a little extra decoration to her dress. 'As Miss Holmes walked up the aisle between desks with a smart blue dress on, David got a pen full of ink and flicked it onto the back of her dress. She never knew it was him as the ink blended in with the colour of the dress.'

Olwen encouraged the artistic side in her offspring.

David was always the form clown and his high-spirited partnership with Mike Weedon made sure both boys were regularly in trouble with some teachers. 'We were always getting separated because of our antics,' recalls Mike Weedon. 'Every lesson seemed to begin with, "White, get down to the front of the class. Weedon, get to the back of the class." We always tried to sit next to each other, but we played up too much.'

Certainly Miss Holmes did not always fully appreciate David's irrepressible sense of fun. She once caned him in front of the class, and caned him very hard and on his wrist as well as his hand.

Mike Weedon says: 'She was so mad at something he had done she struck him haphazardly across the wrist and we couldn't believe it when David turned round and said, "I'm going to report you to the headmaster." And he went right along to the headmaster, Mr Maurice Hackett. Huge weals had come up on his wrist and he just stormed out of the classroom and into the head's office. She got into trouble and was told to ease off by the head. She missed his hand and hit his wrist and it could have been quite damaging.' David was never shy at sticking up

David during his early years.

for himself. He was well below average height but somehow his energy and his ready wit meant that he was rarely picked on by bigger boys.

David certainly did not shine in his first years at school. He was painfully shy and in his early teens lacked any sort of confidence in himself. But a perceptive and thoughtful teacher helped him to develop. David said, 'When I first started at school I was not very bright

David was always the form clown.

and I did not do very well. I always seemed to be very backward. Then I found that there was something I could do well and that helped me a lot. I was always very physical and we had a very good young teacher, called Mr Joy, who taught us Gymnastics. Because I was agile and could do things he said, "That is very good" and he told the rest of the class to watch how I did one exercise and try to copy it.'

David had never before been used as a model for his contemporaries to match, and he thoroughly enjoyed the experience. 'It was the first time a teacher had ever said anything like that to me. That was a big turning point for me, because I thought if I can do that in Gymnastics, why can't I do it in History or Geography or whatever.

'I was never very good at Maths but at English and Science I began to creep up the scale because I realised that if I could do something well physically it gave me a spur. Before then I believe that deep down I had sub-consciously given up. I always used to feel the lessons were so complicated and I would just give up before I started so I was always bottom of the class. But Mr Joy proved that I could do something well. That gave me enormous confidence and it opened the door for me. I was a natural gymnast and it has been with me ever since.

'He started me reading a lot and helped me in every way. I worked at science and got an award, and I went on to become a prefect, and captain of the football and swimming teams. I owe that man a lot. At school I was a well-known joker and the reason why was because I was very small and very slight and in order to survive I started clowning. I think this is true of a lot of people who are in comedy.'

David was always able to laugh off his lack of inches but just sometimes he did yearn to be tall. He often looked smaller than he was because he was swallowed by clothes provided just that bit too large to give long-lasting value. 'We never had much money in our family,' he said. 'Everything I owned my mother would say, 'He'll grow into it,' so I had jackets with sleeves that were too long and shoes that were too big. And one Christmas when I was 10 or 11, the thing I wanted more than anything was a bike. Come Christmas morning and there it was. But my feet wouldn't reach the pedals.

'As usual my mother had bought me a full-sized model, "to grow into". My father had to put wooden blocks on the pedals and even then my toes only just touched them. My street cred really plummeted after that.'

A third youngster, Brian Barneycoat or 'Bodgy', became friendly with the young pair and the trio became great pals for many years. David led the threesome on a trip into central London to see his radio heroes The Goons. Peter Sellers was David's childhood idol.

The intrepid threesome all shared a lack of inches. They were all very short for their age all the way through school but never deeply worried. 'We used to call ourselves The Shorthouses,' laughed Mike Weedon. 'I got picked on a couple of times because of my size but David was so funny and well liked I don't think he ever got picked on.'

But perhaps the event which really shaped the future came when David was 14, just after his mother had broken the news to him about his dead twin. The school play had a problem when a young actor dropped out with measles and headmaster Hackett was looking around for a replacement. David remembers, 'For some reason he decided I could do this part. I can still hear him saying, "White, I want a word with you." I thought, "Oh Gawd, what have I done now. This is it. I must be in trouble again." '

But in fact the head carried the news that the boy's illness would keep him out of the production and cheeky young David White was his choice for replacement. 'I want you to take over,' he told David. Perhaps surprisingly, the suggestion was not then a welcome one. David might have enjoyed dressing up and larking about at home but doing it in public before the critical eyes of his pals was quite another thing. 'I wasn't very keen at all,' he says. 'I thought acting and plays were girls' things. When you're in a working class school being in a play seems like playing girls' games. You don't fancy doing it because it's all a bit girlish and I most definitely wanted to be seen as one of the lads.'

But the headmaster insisted. 'I think you would be absolutely right and you are the only one I can think of to do this part,' he said firmly. With that he left young David White to cogitate on his first troublesome casting problem. 'I was standing there for about five minutes trying to work out what he had said,' remembered David. 'Of course, I worked out that I was going to do it anyway. The difference was that he was asking me to do it. I slowly realised that if I said "No" he was going to tell me to do it.'

The play was a one-act production called *Wayside War*, set during the time of the Cromwellian Wars. David entered the action with a heavy heart: 'I was playing a cavalier and dressing up in all those funny clothes made it even worse. But something happened to me when I started to do it. It was somehow amazing. It was fun. It worked. After all that pressure to take part I found to my complete surprise that I was actually enjoying myself.

'I was a natural gymnast.'

'It was a spy story, based on real events which really intrigued me. For the first time it made history come alive for me. And being on stage was an amazing experience.

'We did it for three nights. Our parents and friends all came and it went down really well. Just being in the play was amazing. I can remember the audience laughing and I really, really enjoyed it. It was a way of being clever and a success, and I'd never been much of either in school.'

David's mother was impressed. She said, 'We knew he had something special. He had this quick way with him that could lift people in the audience. I think it comes from our family. Back in Wales our family would always provide their own entertainment. Everyone stood up and did a turn, going back generations.'

The stage success gave young David confidence but he still had no thought of acting becoming a career. 'I don't think I gave a second thought to taking it that seriously,' said David. 'I was much too busy having a good time.' The teenage trio enjoyed their own company and after school would rush off on their bicycles on

With his childhood friends Mike Weedon and Brian Barneycoat.

trips into the green countryside on the very edge of London. At weekends they would cycle to Broxbourne to secret dens they made on the banks of the River Lea.

But baiting teachers with practical jokes and at all costs avoiding taking schoolwork too seriously did not endear the trio to the school authorities. Headmaster Hackett was concerned, as the boys approached 15, that their childish pranks could turn into more serious teenage trouble-making, and wisely decided that perhaps they needed a more creative outlet for their energy and mischief. Recognising David's considerable dramatic skill and potential ability to act he sent off David and Mike with another problem boy to Douglas Weatherhead, then the drama instructor for Middlesex who was running an evening drama group attached to the local amateur Incognito Theatre Group.

'When you're in a working class school being in a play seems like playing girls' games.'

'I've got three boys here and if they don't find themselves something to do they're going to get themselves into trouble,' said the headmaster to the amiable Mr Weatherhead.

He recalled fondly, 'Right from the start I could see that David was quite obviously a winner. Mike Weedon was quite reasonable but David, you could see from the start, was simply exceptional. He picked up accents and intonations beautifully. He would have been a very good serious actor, but of course his lack of height went against him. In those days you had to be the classic tall and good-looking Laurence Olivier type to get anywhere.'

David recalls that his initial euphoria for acting with the Incognitos was not totally based upon dramatic ambition. 'We went down there for the first time one Monday night because we were now inflamed with the success of *Wayside War*. And we found that there were 22 girls there and one bloke. We thought, "Yeah, we'll have some of that."

'We used to go on Mondays and Wednesdays and it quickly became much more than a hobby for me. It gradually became more and more fascinating and more and more interesting. The more I found out about acting the more interesting it became.

'I never found acting an easy thing to do. It was difficult, very difficult. But because it was so difficult it became a question of developing dedication and application to try to keep improving and developing my skills. And I learned early on that the only person who can really do all that is yourself. I tried to learn and absorb from people who knew more than me, from teachers, directors, actors or anyone, and I tried to apply that knowledge in every way I could.'

'It was a way of being clever and a success, and I'd never been much of either in school.'

Part of David's initial audition for the Incognitos was to pretend to be much older, first 45 and then 85. Most youngsters of his age would scarcely have appreciated the difference and been inclined to bend every joint stiff to simulate either middle age or old age. But David, observers recall, was able, apparently effortlessly, to suggest the difference.

'David was a natural,' says Douglas Weatherhead. 'He took to acting like a duck to water. And he always kept us in fits of laughter. Whenever we took a break for coffee he kept the whole thing going. I never did find out what sort of trouble the headmaster thought he was heading for but once he found an outlet in acting there was no sign of any trouble for him. That was it. He was wide-eyed with enthusiasm when he arrived.'

The diminutive trio remained good friends long after they left school and, as soon as they were 16, they all exchanged their faithful pushbikes for much more exciting motorbikes which instantly enlarged the scope of their adventures. David's first motorbike was an aged 350cc BSA on which he lavished hours of tender loving care.

His mother was never too keen on her precious son's new obsession, fearing the dangers of David revving around the country on the powerful machine. She was even less enthusiastic when he took the bike to pieces in her tiny hallway. Bitterly cold weather meant that this was the only place to service the bike but Olwen gave David a fierce telling off every time a drop of oil found its way onto her carpet.

The motorbikes changed the lives of the youngsters. Their horizons were suddenly nationwide. All of a sudden from being limited to within a few hours pedalling distance of their homes they could now explore the whole country. With David leading the way on his powerful 350cc machine with Brian Barneycoat riding pillion and Mike following on his smaller 250cc bike they set out to explore the beauties of Britain.

Despite his enthusiasm for high speed David was usually a careful motorcyclist, yet he did come close to losing his life on his motorbike when he was racing back from Clacton, with Mike Weedon riding pillion. David had picked a favourite personal short-cut winding round a sequence of back roads. As dusk fell the two youngsters thrilled to the speedy journey and leaned energetically into every bend, until they reached a particularly sharp corner

Opposite page:
David's mother knew she had something special when she saw him in his first school play. She could never have known that years later he would front the most popular comedy series ever. He is shown here with co-stars Lennard Pearce and Nicholas Lyndhurst.

when David yelled to his passenger: 'There's too much gravel, I'm going to lose it.'

To Mike's terror David pulled out of the bend, straightened the screaming machine and went dead ahead on over the bank at the side of the road. With enormous good fortune they crashed violently through the undergrowth and found the road again on the other side. They hit the bank and the bike just took

> **'David, you could see from the start, was simply exceptional.'**

off. When they landed again they were remarkably lucky to hit the road facing straight ahead and carry on unscathed. Mike breathlessly yelled to his daring driver: 'Dave, Dave, stop. Let's have a fag.'

But the daring young man on his flying machine was seriously scared himself. He yelled back grimly: 'If I stop now I'll lose my nerve,' and just kept on heading for home.

David's love of speed was undimmed by the experience. He later exchanged his trusty 350cc BSA for a much more powerful 500cc Shooting Star which could comfortably exceed the magical 'ton'. Mike Weedon recalls: 'He really cherished that 500. He did the ton more than once. He loved high speed. He used to get quite excited about having gone more than 100mph. We had no farings to make us more streamlined in those days. David would lie down as flat as he could on the bike to get up to those sorts of speeds. He loved it. We used to race each other up the A1 and back down the Watford by-pass.'

David insists: 'We were never real tearaways on the bikes, we were gentleman motorcyclists. There were the rockers but me and my mates had flat caps and goggles and we weren't into all the Teddy Boy thing either. We were very shy and found it very difficult to talk to the ladies and we didn't succeed in that department at all. So we concentrated on our motorbikes. I suppose that is what young lads do – find other ways to expend their energy. We used to strip them down, heat them up, and rebuild them.

'I was so into motorbikes that in our outside toilet on the toilet roll holder was carved something like 'While You Sit Here You Will Have All Your Best Dreams'. And I wrote underneath 'Or A Super Road Rocket.' At the time that was the Mercedes Benz of motorbiking.'

David was the first of the trio to take much of an interest in the opposite sex although he was always careful to make sure that girls never came between him and his motorbike. He was always close to girl next door, Julie Pressland, who was just three years younger. She says: 'He was always so single-minded that what he wanted to do was to make it as an actor. There was never any room for a serious romance. He was so dedicated to making it that nothing was going to get in his way. I think he always thought, deep down, that you could either have a normal family life, a marriage and children and all that or you could be a successful actor. Not both. He felt if you tried to carry a wife and children along as an actor they would somehow fall by the wayside.'

When he left school David was wary of following his brother into the precarious existence of struggling as a would-be actor. David agreed to follow his parents' considered advice that he should get a trade behind him first. His forceful mother Olwen typically insisted: 'Actin'? That's not respectable. You need a job. You need a trade.'

David's first job was as an apprentice garage mechanic but he hated 'lying under cars in mid-winter, stuff dropping on you, the wind whistling up your bum.' He left after a year and decided to train as an electrician, while still pursuing his acting interests on an unpaid basis. He joined the London Electricity Board as an apprentice but the Board made him redundant. 'I was 20 when I was made redundant by the LEB,' he recalls. 'It was awful.'

David decided if no one else would employ him he would have to work for himself and with friend Bob Bevil set up B and W Installations. But David sums up in one word his efforts to become a businessman: 'Pathetic. I was doing so much acting, I was always having to take time off from work.

'Then one day I got an offer to go to drama school. I was about 21 and well into amateur dramatics. I was spending every night of the week in the theatre. I was working during the day and more or less every night I would be down at the theatre. Then I won this award and the adjudicator said, "I would never recommend anyone to take up the theatre but there is one man who has a possibility of making a career out of it," and he named me. My head was so big I couldn't get out of the room. I was absolutely over the moon.

'I tried to learn and absorb from people who knew more than me.'

'But at the time I was sort of engaged to this girl. My young lady lived in Lea Green, the other side of Lewisham, which is the other side of London from my home in North Finchley. It was a long way late at night in the rain. I used to take her home on my motorbike so you can tell how besotted I was, and then I had to turn round and come back home.

'I had not bought her a ring but we were unofficially engaged. We were just waiting for her 18th birthday to announce it. On the journey to her house that night of the award I was full of it and I said to her, "What do you think? Perhaps I could become an actor."

'There was no reply at first and then she said, "Look if you want to be an actor, you go and be an actor, but don't think you are going to marry me. You're not. That is not what I want out of life. I want a man who is going to come home and spend a certain amount of time there. I want a husband, a two up and two down house, a steady income and a family. I want a reliable chap with a steady income, a car, a couple of kids."

'So much for love. Anyway, I was so terribly in love with this girl that I didn't want to go to drama school because I wanted to get married to her. I gave up the idea of becoming a professional actor. I was more interested in her at the time. But that sowed the seed and because I was totally involved as an amateur actor and no one was going to take that away from me I went back to being a happy amateur. Within a year we had a terrible row, and we split up. I have never seen her since. I only know from a friend of mine that she did eventually get married many, many years ago. Really the split was not over what she said, exactly, but it was a catalyst.

'By the time I was 23 I knew I was no longer going to get married. I would get close to girls and then have this fear of being tied down. It gradually became more apparent to me that I could have a go at acting and if I wasn't really any good I could go back to being an electrician. I couldn't bear the thought of reaching 35 without having had a shot at what I really wanted. I started to think, "Right – this is the time. I have no ties. I must have a go at being an actor." If I didn't I knew I would never forgive myself.'

Working with the Incognitos was certainly good training at putting on the show with a minimum of backing. The energetic Douglas Weatherhead had his young team travelling all over London by public transport just for the chance of competing in as many drama festivals as possible. 'David never minded hard work,' says Douglas. 'Once we had to take all our props to the other side of London on the bus. I remember David and I struggling up the narrow and awkward spiral staircase onto the top deck of a double decker with a Welsh dresser. We just laughed about it all.'

David was always desperately eager to get on stage and one evening in his enthusiasm he walked into a jagged piece of corrugated iron on one of the ramshackle buildings outside. He staggered into the tiny theatre with blood pouring from his head and said, 'I've had a bit of a bang.'

Amateur actress Vera Neck said, 'David would never walk if he could run anywhere. He came in bleeding from this nasty gash on his forehead and he dripped blood all over the stage for the rest of the evening. We all felt he should go and have stitches but he wasn't going to let a little thing like that make him miss his rehearsals. He was always supremely careless about his appearance so blood gushing down his shirt was nothing out of the ordinary.'

David would often race to rehearsals straight from work and sometimes his grubby clothes raised eyebrows among the more senior and established members of the Incognitos. Vera Neck says, 'He sometimes turned up in dirty, grubby things. I remember being shocked at the colour of his underpants when we were rehearsing one of those "Sailor Beware" things and he had to drop his trousers.

'There were all these elderly ladies among the cast – I suppose he was about 20 and we were 30 something – and they went "Tut-tut-tut-tut". His pants were every colour of the rainbow but you could see an underlying grey. And he couldn't blame his mum. She used to "do" for me and she was a clean little body. But I'll never forget those grubby underpants. The play had a bit of rough and tumble and he disappeared over the back of a couch with his bum in the air. He had these psychedelic patterned pants with an underlying grey hue. We matronly types all went "Dear, dear, dear, dear!"'

With enormous good fortune, they crashed violently through the undergrowth and found the road again on the other side.

David was also honest enough to admit later that during those early stages of his amateur career, 'I really didn't think I had the ability to turn professional. Most people who become actors are so confident. They know for certain that they are right and everybody else is wrong. I was the opposite. I was very, very insecure – mind you, I think I'm still insecure but I'm not as bad as I was.'

David's 21st birthday party was an occasion for the White family to really push the boat out. In order to cram in as many guests as possible on David's big day they took off all the downstairs doors to make more space. David prepared much of the sumptuous spread himself and the music of Johnny Tillotson, Elvis Presley and the Everly Brothers rang out down Lodge Lane. 'It was a wonderful party,' remembers Julie Pressland. 'We all thought it was great having an open-plan house.

'I went to David's house a lot at that time. Me and David and his partner Bob Bevil and my friend Carol Haddock used to go to our local dance hall, the Atheneum in Muswell Hill or up to Alexandra Palace for a drink and then come back to David's.

'We'd sit in his front room and talk and talk for hours on end. He had such plans and ambitions for the future, he just loved everything about acting and drama, he was so very determined to be good at every part he had. We were a foursome for a time but David and I never had a romance. I did have a crush on David but that was when I was five or six. He was literally the boy next door, a great pal.

What he wanted to do was make it as an actor – there was never any room for a serious romance.

'That was when I began to notice a more serious side. He was still great fun and often he would be larking about of course, just like before. But also he would sometimes recite long bits of poetry or quotations from Shakespeare. He was becoming very well read and getting more and more into his acting. It seemed to dominate his whole life. He loved Richard Burton and his recording of *Under Milk Wood* in that wonderful voice.

The young David would grow up to be counted amongst the funniest faces on television. He is shown here with laughtermakers Les Dawson, Des O'Connor, Bruce Forsyth and Ruby Wax.

David could copy that voice brilliantly and the Welsh in him really seemed to come out. We all knew then that he had an amazing God-given talent.

'David had all the typical motorbike leather gear but when he went out in the evening in his suit and tie he always looked impeccable. He had this gorgeous thick wavy hair and that cheeky grin. But even more he had this remarkable personality where he could walk into a pub and just make everyone laugh.

'It seemed so effortless. He could instantly have people eating out of his hand. It was obvious to me that he was going to do much more with his life than mend fuses. He always made jokes about not being very tall. I remember once he couldn't get served in our local, The Torrington at the end of Lodge Lane, so he stood on the bar rail and just held his money out for a giggle. He didn't mind everyone laughing at him being small, he stood up there to make us all laugh.'

'I was working during the day, and more or less every night I would be down at the theatre.'

Julie herself got a shock the night David came home rather late from another hugely successful night with the Incognitos. She recalls: 'I was 22 at the time and he gave me the fright of my life. I used to sleep in our front bedroom and I was woken up about three o'clock one morning by what I thought was the sound of someone trying to break into one of the houses. I looked out and it was David standing all forlorn with his toolbag. I opened the window as quietly as I could and he said that he was very late home from doing a play and his mum had locked him out.

'I went downstairs and brought him through our house so he could climb

23

over the fence and get in the back way. I was frightened because I was in my nightie and my mum and dad were asleep. I kept telling him to be quiet and he kept giggling and larking about. Then when I got him outside he got on top of the fence and of all things he started reciting the balcony scene from *Romeo and Juliet*. I was really panicking by then because I knew if my mum came downstairs and found David there with me in my nightclothes she would never believe that I was just helping him to get home. I said, "For God's sake shut up, if my mum and dad hear you, we'll both be dead." But that was so typical of his humour, he always had a tremendous amount of fun in him.

'We got on very well together and we were always amazed that our mothers also got on really well. Because while David's mum was very broad Welsh my mum was just as broad Irish. They both had really strong accents and they used to have these incredible conversations. David used to say that the only reason they never rowed with each other was because they each did not have a clue what the other one was saying.

'In our growing up years everybody liked David. He was always very funny with a natural gentle humour that was never directed at anyone but himself. I know they say most people who are very funny are usually manic depressives but David never was. You never saw him depressed or down. He just had a natural sunny good nature.

'David was always very generous. He was one of the first of his contemporaries in Lodge Lane to get a car, a little mini-van that he and Bob used for their business. He was always ready to use it to help people out. When Ernie Pressland's baby daughter Sarah was suddenly taken ill with a racing heart David rushed her and Ernie's wife Claire to hospital. Ernie is still grateful: 'Even in those days they were homing in on potential cot deaths. My mother knew there was something wrong with Sarah because she had had two youngsters die herself. I was at work at the time and David took the wife and the baby up to Whittington Hospital. They wanted to get her there as fast as possible and it was just as well David was around to help.

'It turned out Sarah was born with two little pacemakers in her heart instead of one. Every so often something will trigger off the second one and her heart

'I couldn't bear the thought of reaching the age of thirty-five without having a shot at what I really wanted.'

would go ten to the dozen and she got a loss of blood pressure. She is fine now and has a baby son of her own called Daniel. We will always be grateful to David.'

David was in action again with his makeshift ambulance when Ernie's and Julie's sister Maureen needed rushing to hospital to have her baby. And to complete the job he took Maureen's husband Rob to bring her and the baby home.

Yet on arriving for the return trip David could not resist a joke. As Maureen was coming out of the ward with the nurse who was holding the baby David and Rob were approaching down a long corridor. Suddenly David brushed past Rob and shouted, 'Now we'll see whose baby this is!'

It took Maureen and Rob a moment but they did quickly realise this was a typical David White laugh. The nurse was not so experienced in this curiously quirky sense of humour and almost dropped the baby.

Opposite page:
A Larkin family snap!

CHAPTER TWO

Dramatics

*I*t did not take long for the Incognitos to realise that their little amateur group was witnessing some highly professional performances from young David White. In his early 20s David was reaching remarkable heights in the world of north London amateur dramatics. David was 24 when he produced what many contemporaries agree was his finest dramatic performance, in Winter Journey *by Clifford Odets. It was not his usual comic turn but the highly charged role of a tough New York theatrical director forcing one more decent role out of a crumpled and drunken actor.*

David's director Christopher Webb recalls, 'The part was played in the West End by Michael Redgrave. It called for David to really put this poor actor through it. The guy is really on his beam ends when David's character blasts him once more into action. We worked very closely together on it for many nights. I pushed him very hard over and over again because I knew he had a fine performance in him. There was a real clash of wills. There is nothing like actors having a bit of hatred for their director to inspire that bit extra from them.

'We used to rehearse in empty schoolrooms and I would allow a small number of people to come and watch. I convinced David that he had to be really worked up when the scene started. I got him working on his breathing and really pumping himself up before we even started. One particular night there was a real excitement in the air and when he launched into his tirade against this other actor the atmosphere was absolutely electric.

David generated such force and willpower it was almost overwhelming.

'The scene was quite spell-binding. One or two of the girls in the tiny audience were in tears as David generated such force and will power it was almost overwhelming. It was amazing, quite brilliant. I think that was when he really decided to he had it in him to make a career of acting.'

Local critic Bill Gelder was impressed enough to announce to the readers of Finchley and Barnet: 'So far as the acting was concerned, there were three performances good enough to be judged by the highest amateur standards. Indeed, that by David White might be said without flattery to be in a professional class, it was done with such verve and explosive force. Mr White made his

Opposite page: David's big TV break was in *Do Not Adjust Your Set!* He is shown here with his co-stars, the future Pythons Michael Palin, Terry Jones and Eric Idle.

reputation with the Incognitos and is one of the comparatively few amateurs whom I could conscientiously recommend for the professional theatre.

'He has a brother there already (it must run in the family) but chooses instead, and perhaps wisely, to earn a steady living as an electrical engineer, devoting any surplus high-voltage energy to the interests of the local stage. Without pushing the electrical metaphor too hard, he gave a dynamic performance as the producer of the play within the play.'

Shortly after his success in *Winter Journey*, David had a crucial piece of good fortune. The push that he needed to turn professional came courtesy of his brother Arthur, who had landed a role in the Noel Coward play *South Sea Bubble* at Bromley. Arthur was working with director Simon Oates, an old friend, and was busy rehearsing the small but potentially amusing role of a comical coloured butler. At the last minute Arthur was offered a much sought-after television job with the BBC's trail-blazing crime series *Z-Cars* and he begged his pal to be released from the agreement.

David with (left to right) his Aunt Edie, his brother Arthur, his mother Olwen and his father Arthur.

Simon Oates recalls, 'Arthur told me, "My brother wants to be an actor" so I went to see David at the Manor Players in Finchley playing Paul of Tarsus in *A Man Born To Be King*. It wasn't much to do with comedy but I could see right away that he was stunningly talented.'

Afterwards Simon approached David and asked: 'I hear you want to turn pro.' 'Yes, I do,' answered David immediately. 'Well make your mind up,' said the director. David did not need any time to consider the offer. It was the chance he had been waiting for. He made his mind up there and then.

In spite of his mother's woeful warnings he gave his share of the ailing electrical business to his partner in exchange for the company's Mini van and joined Bromley Rep. 'I said yes to the offer of course,' said David. 'But I was terrified. There are certain moments in your life – like the first time you have sex, I suppose – which you can never recreate. You can't breathe with the excitement of it. I was being paid fifteen quid a week and I couldn't believe they were giving me money for something I would have done for nothing.'

> **Afterwards Simon approached David and said, 'I hear you want to turn pro.'**

Simon Oates recalls, 'He had to put a bit of brown make-up on for the part as he was supposed to be a South Sea Islander. It wasn't a large part but you could see his comic potential. He was just naturally funny. There was a great big talent there waiting to be honed. He made me cry with laughter.'

Of David's first paid performance on April 5, 1965, the *Bromley and Kentish Times* recorded solemnly at the time: 'A small, but well acted part is that of David White as the native butler of the governor.' A remarkable comedy career had begun. Oates says: 'He did go back to Bromley after the week-long run of the play. I suggested he should be taken on by the company and he was.'

David might have landed his first paid engagement but he still did not possess that essential actor's accessory, an agent. His brother Arthur was asked by old friend Malcolm Taylor, an actor who was trying to move into production, to take a part in a new run of *Under Milk Wood* which was to be staged at the Vanbrugh Theatre, the London headquarters of the famous Royal Academy of Dramatic Art. Arthur turned the job down saying he was not available, but he suggested his younger brother. Malcolm Taylor was not too impressed by the thought. He said: 'Well, it's very kind of you Arthur but I don't really want amateurs.'

David had done only the one paid job by then but in spite of his obvious lack of experience Malcolm Taylor agreed to see him. Taylor recalls, 'I relented in the end and thought it wouldn't do any harm to give Arthur's brother an audition. He came round to my flat in Maida Vale and I will always remember him sitting, shaking with fear, on my sofa. But as soon as he opened his mouth to do the part I knew that he had real talent. He got the job.'

David said, 'I had no work at the time. I would have done anything if it was in the theatre. This bloke asked me to go down and audition, which I did, and he gave me the part. We played for four weeks in the Vanbrugh for something like £5 a week and split the box office. At the end of four weeks I think we all earned about £30 which wasn't as bad as it sounds in those days when you haven't got a family or any responsibilities, and you haven't got a car and you're living at home. And it was a wonderful opportunity.'

David was best man at the wedding of his friend Malcolm Taylor. It was a predictably laughter-packed affair.

It most certainly was, because in the audience on one evening early in the run was an eager young agent called Ann Callender, a junior partner with the Richard Stone organisation. Ann was there with her actor-turned-writer husband David Croft, a multi-talented man destined to become the BBC's comedy stalwart with a string of successes including *Dad's Army, Are you Being Served?, It 'Ain't 'Alf Hot, Mum, Hi de Hi* and *'Allo, 'Allo.*

Ann Callender remembers, 'I was completely taken by this young man who seemed unbelievably talented and really rather exceptional. David White was just so funny I had to try to sign him up.'

On the following Monday David kept an appointment with Ann Callender in the impressive offices of the Richard Stone agency. She says, 'There was no question about his talent. Everyone who saw him in *Under Milk Wood* must have

'David White was just so funny I had to try and sign him up.'

noticed it. He was absolutely brilliant. He came and saw me and we had a long chat and I did in fact become his agent.'

David's second play at Bromley was *Diplomatic Baggage* and if his new reputation for getting laughs was not already irrevocably established at the end of his first production it most certainly was by the close of the second.

David remembers these formative days in precise detail. '*Diplomatic Baggage* was a farce, a good old typically British farce,' he recalls. 'I was a waiter again and there was this important scene where I had to come in to this hotel room where there was a bloke with two girls in a state of undress.

'The bloke orders a meal and as the waiter I deliver his food on this trolley with a tablecloth right down to the ground. "Leave the meal," says the bloke and I leave. Then he finds out that his wife is coming so he is desperate to find somewhere to hide the girls. He gets the two girls to hide in the bottom of the trolley, hidden by the tablecloth. Then he calls the waiter back to take away this trolley.

'Now my waiter had been messed about all day and by this time he was pretty fed-up. So he comes in and grabs the trolley and has to pull it away thinking it was the same weight as before when he has pushed it in. The audience knows of course that it is much heavier with the weight of the girls. I went to walk away pulling the trolley.

'The stage directions were what you might call pretty minimal, they just said, "The trolley is now much heavier and he falls over." My idea for conveying that sort of grew from rehearsals but when it came to it with all the excitement of the first night I just really went for it much bigger than I would normally have done.

'That's your job from now on. You are the comedy man from now.'

'As I pulled the trolley, I did an exaggerated version of what I thought would really happen, my feet went from under me and I flew up into the air up to being horizontal and then fell straight down on the floor. It doesn't sound that much when you describe it in words but when it happened the audience went hysterical. It brought the house down. Being physically adept it was not that difficult for me, I thought it was quite natural. But the audience went on laughing and clapping for about five minutes afterwards.

'And I went further. I had the waiter get up, not understanding why the trolley would not move. I walked round the trolley and stared at it suspiciously. On top was a huge silver dish with a big lid. I quickly whipped it off as if suspecting there was some incredibly heavy food under there. The audience found what they thought was going through the waiter's head really amusing and they just kept laughing and laughing.

'By then everybody in the rest of the cast was looking at me. We've been stopped now for maybe 10 minutes and the audience is still laughing fit to bust.

'I was just a little unknown and I was just doing what came naturally. I did a little bit more and then eventually I thought, "Blimey, I'll have to take this trolley off sometime," and I made my much delayed exit.

'Afterwards the director came up to me and I thought I was going to get this almighty bollocking but instead he just kept saying, "Wonderful, brilliant, fantastic. That's your job from now on. You are the comedy man now." '

David was taken on at Bromley Rep as their last contracted artist and he says, 'I spent my entire time either learning words or rehearsing or doing a show.

I was living, breathing, eating, sleeping, talking, thinking a show. The theatre completely took over my life and I loved it. It was terribly exciting and terribly rewarding for someone from my background with no training to be involved with real actors. It was wonderful. Absolutely wonderful.'

Following his brother into the acting business was a decision that far from delighted his parents. David said afterwards, 'The day we told Dad we wanted to become actors he was shattered. "Why give up worthwhile trades and waste your lives?"'

David knew he would always regret it if he did not take his big chance. He was unhappy as an electrician and believed he had it in him to become a professional actor. But at the ripe old age of 25 he was still cautious enough to set conditions. 'I gave myself a time limit. If I wasn't earning a good living by 30 I would return to my old trade. They were terrible years but by then I was besotted with the stage.'

Now he had a new career, David White found he needed a new name. He said:

Now he had a new career, David White found he needed a new name.

'When I got my job in the theatre I got three Equity members to sign my contract so that I could join Equity and sent the form off. But they phoned me up and said I couldn't have the name David White as there was already another actor registered with Equity with that name. They don't allow two actors to use the same name as it would be confusing.

'The woman from Equity said she could do the change over the phone, so I was on the spot, I had to decide on a new name there and then. First of all I said I'll just extend my name and become David Whitehead. She said that name was already being used as well. She asked, "Is there any other name?" What popped into my mind was Jason. I suggested David Jason and she went away and then came back and said, "That's all right." All of a sudden I was David Jason.'

Ann Callender set about finding work for her young hopeful in earnest but she was not helped by David's shy disposition. 'David was never a socialite, he did not like being paraded and he was not very keen on anything about that traditional slave market that an agency used to be. We got on terribly well and had loads of meetings about his career but there weren't many social occasions.

'He was very shy with girls. He spent a long time with Michelle Dotrice and in fact I thought he would probably end up marrying her, but in the end it did not come to anything.'

But David was learning about the business perhaps faster than his agent realised. Today top comedian Bob Monkhouse is a friend and a fan of David Jason but he recalls the time when the young wannabe was a handful to work with. Bob Monkhouse cheerfully recalled: 'It was back in 1971 when I met him. I had never heard of David Jason and I went to see a show called *She's Done It Again!* with Brian Rix playing the part of a vicar whose wife has just had sextuplets. It was a very old farce, written for Robertson Hare. I was to take over from Brian. I met David during rehearsal and loved him on sight.

'We opened at the Playhouse, Weston-super-Mare, and for me it was like being hit between the eyes with a sledgehammer. I went out there to get laughs and there was no way anyone could get laughs apart from David. He was hysterical. He was acrobatic. He was wearing this white wig, with a white moustache and beard. He looked like a little old man. Everything about him was 70, except these incredible acrobatics and falls and amazing bits of business which all appeared on the night.

'We had never seen it at rehearsals but, on the night, suddenly his foot was jammed between the cushions on the couch and he couldn't get it out and there was five minutes of hysterical laughter and the other foot went in. He was just wonderful. He tumbled everywhere and the people adored him. And who was best at the end of the show? When we walked down, he walked down before me and the roof lifted off. Then I walked down as the star of the thing and everyone went quiet.

'David used to crack me up. There was one scene where he had to come to me with the sixth and final baby in a crib. He had to come running in and give it to me. Well, the things he put in that crib that the audience couldn't see. First of all there was the baby, then he had a horror mask on the baby, horrible lolling eyes and tongue hanging out all bloody. Then he started doing obscene things with the baby. I won't go into details but it involved the use of a frankfurter sausage and a lot of ketchup. Eventually I used to dread this crib coming out for fear of what he had put in it. He even put all my underwear in it one time. And I still had to look in and say 'What a beautiful baby!' I think it was the funniest, happiest summer season, because of David, that I have ever had.'

David's agent could see her bashful young client needed a television chance and she turned to rising young comedy producer Humphrey Barclay as the man to provide it. She wrote to Barclay just at the time he was moving from radio to join the London ITV station Rediffusion to begin working on a completely new comedy strand.

Barclay remembers, 'I had just left radio and landed this job in television and for the first time I was actually a television producer. I was very new and very nervous and I was charged with putting together a children's comedy show. We had already got Eric Idle, Michael Palin and Terry Jones who were fine but they were all very cerebral and university-like. I was looking for someone who could provide some contrast.

'I approached Malcolm Taylor. He auditioned and was very jolly and good fun but he said, "You don't want me, you want my friend David Jason."'

David is still grateful to his friend. 'It was a fantastically generous thing for Malcolm to do,' he said. 'He knew Humphrey was after a little comedy actor with a great range and was kind enough to think of me. He explained to Humphrey that I was working on the end of the pier in Bournemouth with Dick Emery and

David's agent could see that her bashful young client needed a television chance.

Humphrey telephoned me and asked could he come down and see the show. I said, "Wonderful". I was doing very small parts in two plays back to back and one of them was doing absolutely nothing. The better one was *Chase Me Comrade*, another typical old English farce.'

David did not make his big entrance until midway through the second half and Barclay, the thoughtful former classics graduate from Trinity College, Cambridge, sat surrounded by guffawing holidaymakers who were thoroughly enjoying Dick Emery cavorting about the stage in drag. As the evening wore on

and David Jason continued to fail to emerge, Barclay was beginning to gaze yearningly at the exit.

Eventually the moment arrived. It was a vital time in David Jason's young life and he recalls, 'For the first time in my career I went "anti" the director. I really just followed my own instincts. My character, Bobby Hargreaves the next door neighbour who has just moved in, had to come on stage at a point in the play when everyone else has disappeared. The others are all chasing this guy dressed up as this Russian ballerina or whatever, and I am trying to find out if there is anybody in the house.

'**For the first time in my career I went anti the director.**'

'At the bottom of the stairs there is a ship's bell. I have the entire stage to myself and I have to ring the bell which is the signal for everyone else to rush back on stage. Every time I cross the stage in my search I run past the bell and look at it significantly. I think about ringing it and I even make as if to ring it. This begins to wind up the audience and they start yelling, "Go on ring the bell. Ring it. Ring it." But I make them wait and I drag it out as they are shouting and it started to drive that audience mad.'

In the audience, Humphrey Barclay the mild-mannered former head boy of Harrow School and one-time Cambridge Footlights director, a master of all the

most sophisticated aspects of humour, had completely forgotten all thoughts of leaving early. He was yelling and shouting with the rest of the audience, 'Ring the bell, ring the bell!'

At last David Jason relented and rang the bell. 'Then they really went bananas,' he said. 'They knew what I was going to do. But, you see, in comedy often it is not what you do but when you do it. This is the Laurel and Hardy message. If you watch Laurel and Hardy who have always been one of my faves, you find yourself going, "I know what you're going to do. But when are you going to do it?" I had learned that.

'Humphrey met me afterwards, and he told me, "I really must say that I was thinking of leaving because it was not exactly my scene. But when you came on and did that business with the bell, I have never seen anything like it in my life. You drove that audience to distraction. Even I was yelling 'Ring it, ring it!'"'

Humphrey Barclay recalls: 'I went back into his dressing room and we chatted and he was very down to earth. I swanked about being a television producer and admitted I hadn't done it for long. He said he hadn't long given up being an electrician. And I just knew for sure that he had this magical ability to make people laugh. I asked him if he would be in this TV show I was planning called *Do Not Adjust Your Set* and he turned out to be very, very good in it.'

The young comedy actress Denise Coffey completed the team and *Do Not Adjust Your Set* became an an innovative and successful show. But it did have a most peculiar start. David said: 'There was this wonderful moment when we all met and they told us, "This is a really major opportunity, an amazingly huge project. We want you to do six half-hour revue-type television programmes for kids. It's never been done before. We want you to be more or less adult." The attitude Humphrey Barclay and the other guys had was to treat the audience as we would ourselves. It was quite revolutionary at the time.

> **'I asked him if he would be in this TV show called *Do Not Adjust Your Set*, and he turned out to be very very good in it.'**

'Right at the start Humphrey announced he had to prove to all the powers that be at the station that we were really worth this great investment. He took us all out to lunch and said that we had to go back that afternoon and prove ourselves to be funny.

'He said he had a studio booked and that we had to go in there and be funny. That is the hardest thing on earth with no script or direction or preparation. "How do we do it?" we asked. Humphrey said, "You've got to do it because your future relies upon it." We protested that nobody had prepared anything and Humphrey said, "Yes, that's the idea."

'I thought then that I had walked into a lunatic asylum. I thought it was crazy. We all thought it was mad, and Michael Palin freaked out completely. Anyway we all filed into the studio at Kingsway and we just went...silly. We just went daft. Terry Jones kept on throwing himself backwards off his chair. Every time anybody spoke Terry Jones threw himself off his chair.

'That was all he did and I thought, "I wish I had thought of that." So I threw myself off my chair and then everybody threw themselves off their chairs. So we were all doing it. Then we thought, we can't all do that. That piece of tape would probably be worth a fortune today because we were pathetic. We were rubbish. We had no form and no content. They just said go out there and be funny and we weren't.'

Do Not Adjust Your Set, launched on Boxing Day 1967, was an instant hit with its young audience and plenty of parents tried to get home early enough to join in the zany humour. David recalled, 'It grabbed people with its anarchic humour. Adults would say, "I don't know what you're watching this bloody rubbish for", but the kids loved it.' One of the highlights of each show was David Jason's appearance as special agent Captain Fantastic in a running superhero serial that was deeply absurd. David appeared with Denise Coffey in an unlikely double act and the pair also wrote the scripts.

David always felt a little apart from the three other male stars of *Do Not Adjust Your Set*. After three hugely successful series Messrs Jones, Palin and Idle began a campaign to move the show to a less restricting late-night slot and David says: 'The upshot was that because they weren't allowed to turn our series into a late show they went away and came back a couple or three years later with John Cleese and Graham Chapman and it was called *Monty Python's Flying Circus*. Need I say more?'

David as one of his many characters in *Do not Adjust Your Set!*

'It grabbed people with its anarchic humour. Adults would say "I don't know what you're watching this bloody rubbish for", but the kids loved it.'

The last episode of *Do Not Adjust Your Set* went out on May 14, 1969 and, having been part of such a successful team, David was understandably upset at being excluded from the future comedy plans of Jones, Idle and Palin. Though he wasn't to know it at the time, David posed for a promotional photograph for *Do Not Adjust Your Set* which was to prove painfully prophetic. David and the other three were pictured standing behind a television set which bore the caption 'Ouch!'

David did, however, work with Graham Chapman seven years later in the film *The Odd Job Man*. Chapman played an insurance executive deserted by his wife

David and Nicholas Lyndhurst always enjoyed a good joke during the filming of *Only Fools and Horses*, which served to strengthen their rapport on screen.

and on the brink of suicide. Losing the nerve to kill himself, he hires a weird little oddjob man, played by David, to do it for him.

While the embryonic Pythons set off on their first steps to international stardom David headed in a distinctly different direction, to the mythical Midlands motel that was for so long the setting for the interminable ITV soap opera *Crossroads*.

Ann Callender remembers: 'David did not really want to do it, but at the same time he wanted to learn the television technique for fast turnaround drama. He went into the programme, made up in Birmingham by ATV, as a rather silly gardener type and he was up there for quite a few weeks in spite of his persistent efforts to escape.

'At first he used to say in our frequent telephone conversations, that he had been given a rather dull and tedious person to play. He said the gardener was a very boring character but he accepted that it was very good experience although it was not a very large or interesting role.

'Then after three weeks up there I suddenly had a very angry David on the telephone. He said, "Have you seen the scripts?" I told him that most play scripts were sent to me but not *Crossroads*. He said, "I just can't do this any more. It is completely ridiculous." I did not understand what was going on, I said, "Calm down, David and tell me what is wrong."

'He said, "You know that nice boring little gardener chap I was playing." I said, "Yes, David". He paused and then almost spat down the telephone, "Well he has suddenly turned into some sort of psychopathic killer."' He was incandescent with rage. In the end I said, "Come on, David. You're a professional," and he accepted the situation and said, "Yeah, I'll just get on with it."

'Two or three weeks went by and I did not exactly see the programme every day. It was on while I was still at work and in those days agents did not run to television sets in the office. Then he came on the phone again and my heart sank wondering what was the new problem. He was not earning a great deal of money and he was very punctilious about everything.

'He said, "You won't believe this. I have just had the scripts for the next couple of weeks." I said, "What has happened this time. Are they going to catch you and send you to prison for some dreadful crime." He said, "No, I'm back being a stupid gardener again." He came out of *Crossroads* not very long after that, having learned a very great deal.'

He came out of *Crossroads* not long after that, having learned a great deal.

After *Crossroads*, David did some work in the theatre including a memorable portrayal of Bob Acres in *The Rivals* in the West End which led to his taking over from Michael Crawford in the long-running *No Sex Please – We're British* at the Strand Theatre and then a star role in another comedy *Look No Hans!* at the same theatre.

In *Darling Mr London* he provided Ann Callender with her favourite stage moment. 'David could be a genius of a comic, especially when he was doing physical stunts. One scene involved one of the sofas that turns into a put-you-up bed, which had been put up for obvious reasons. When the husband comes home early David had to dive into this bed which then turned back into a sofa and folded up with him inside. It was a most dangerous and complicated piece of business but David did it brilliantly.'

Digging for gold?

Above:
The house in Buckinghamshire where David spends his time.

Opposite page:
David with Myfanwy Talog, his long-time love who tragically died of cancer.

David Jason readily concedes that luck plays a part in the world of showbusiness. He said, 'I've been up for lots of parts in this business and some of them would surely have changed my whole life and career if I'd got them.'

One such nearly-role was when he was interviewed for and then won the role of Corporal Jones in *Dad's Army*. It was thought that Clive Dunn who had been earmarked for the role would not be available. But two hours later it was discovered that Clive Dunn would be available to play the role after all. David is, however, philosophical about missing out. He said: 'If I had gone into *Dad's Army* then the whole of the rest of my career would have been different. I would probably never have done *Open All Hours* or *Only Fools and Horses*.'

David Jason readily concedes that luck plays a part in the world of showbusiness.

After Malcolm Taylor's generous act of recommendation his friendship with David Jason grew. So much that in 1968 when Taylor married actress Anne Rutter, who had appeared with David in *The Rivals*, he asked David to be best man. It was an invitation that guaranteed laughter all the way.

Taylor recalls, 'The night before the wedding we all went out for a Chinese meal in the Edgware Road and then back to my flat after a very good night out with plenty to drink all round. In the morning I was anxious to make sure everything was ready and I carefully cleaned my shoes. A little later I was surprised that David insisted on cleaning them again though I thought he was just being helpful so I did not protest.

'I did not find out what he was up to until later. It was a top hats and morning suits do in Beaconsfield. And we all got very smartly to the church and as I knelt down at the front at the beginning of the ceremony I could hear all this barely suppressed laughter burbling behind me.

'Of course the he'd only written HE on the instep of my left shoe and LP! on the instep of the right shoe, so when I knelt down I was screaming for help. That was the first thing. Then when we moved into our frightfully middle-class reception on a marquee on the lawn David stood up to make his speech. There was a sprinkling of theatricals there, Sheila Hancock was a guest and so was Frank Windsor as I was directing *Softly, Softly* at the time.

'David got to his feet. Then he stood on a chair so we could all see him clearly. He tipped his hat back and said in a loud, clear voice, "Balls..." I thought my God he's flipped. He is going to lay into the whole ceremony. What on earth is he going to say next? And one of Anne's older relations started to walk out fearing a tirade of abuse.

'He went on in such hilarious style from there my real regret is that I did not think of recording his speech.'

'But before she got very far he went on, "Balls...weddings and christenings are great fun." And we all breathed a huge collective sigh of relief. He went on in such hilarious style from there my real regret is that I did not think of recording his speech. It was a marvellous comedy routine.

'And as if that was not enough, David actually joined us on our honeymoon! We went for a fortnight to Corfu and after the first week David came out on his own and joined us. We were delighted to have him because he was such fun. He loved taking off the Greek waiters doing a whole serving routine in his peculiar version of the Greek language which nobody else could quite understand. The waiters loved it and so did we.'

Opposite page:
Smith, Jones
and Jason!

CHAPTER THREE

Movies & TV

*D*avid Jason is rightly known as Britain's most popular television star. But in his early days as an actor he looked to be heading for a movie career.

David was still largely unknown when he won the role of Nogood Boyo in the film of the Dylan Thomas masterpiece *Under Milk Wood*. David was thrilled because not only was it a major movie but it featured the veritable cream of Welsh acting talent plus three of the world's biggest movie stars of their day – Richard Burton, Peter O'Toole and Elizabeth Taylor.

In such exalted company and in a truly magical film brilliantly directed by Andrew Sinclair, David still managed to give glimpses of his potential, notably in an amusing sequence where Ruth Madoc, later to find fame in *Hi-de-Hi* as the vampish holiday camp Yellowcoat Gladys Pugh, rushes topless into the sea to embrace him. This wonderful film of *Under Milk Wood* has recently been re-mastered as well as issued on video so David's early promise is now there for all to see.

Another very different film, a comedy called *Albert's Follies*, was intended to launch David to the stardom he was clearly destined for. But through no fault of David's, the film proved a bitter disappointment to him. It was a rushed production and made on a very low budget – and it showed.

As usual, David gave it his all, but it cannot have been easy for him because as soon as each day's filming was over he had to make his way from Twickenham through the rush hour traffic to London's West End in time to go on stage at the Strand Theatre in *No Sex Please – We're British*. 'David was working under terrible strain,' says *Albert's Follies* director Ray Selfe, 'because he was doing his very action-packed version of *No Sex Please – We're British*. He must have been pretty exhausted at the end of the day.'

But Ray Selfe had nothing but praise for David in his starring role as a boring civil servant called Albert who dreams of playing out James Bond-style heroics of rescuing girls in distress. 'David was absolutely excellent and contributed

> A comedy called *Albert's Follies* was intended to launch David to the stardom he was clearly destined for.

Opposite page: David feeds the ducks!

Early roles for the
talented young
David Jason.

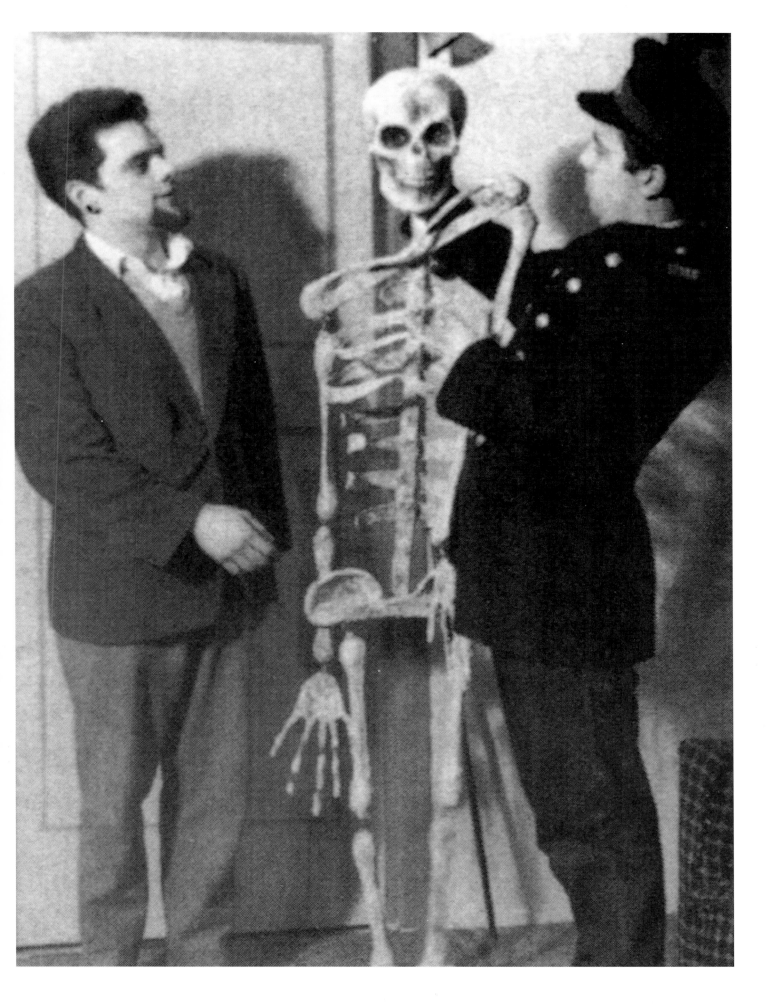

more than 100 per cent,' he said. 'I remember one scene where he had to fall out of a wagon and although he had pads on his elbows and his knees, it was a helluva fall and it required some very agile work from him. He did it so brilliantly the crew gave him a round of applause. David always had such fantastic enthusiasm and a great sense of fun.'

David's next film was *The Odd Job Man* about a man who is simply so perfect that it drives his wife crazy. David had first appeared in *The Odd Job Man* as a half-hour television comedy show with Ronnie Barker who was to become a real comedy mentor and a firm friend in later years. But that film too was a disappointment for David when it veered markedly from the original story.

Perhaps David was always destined to get his big break in TV rather than on the big screen and it came with the starring role in a spy spoof called *The Top Secret Life of Edgar Briggs* with David playing a no-hoper called Edgar who, by a clerical error, is transferred to Counter Espionage at the Ministry of Defence. Appointed Assistant to the Commander, he manages to achieve the most remarkable results despite the fact that he is both stupid and totally unsuited to the job he has been given.

> **They had stunt drivers ready to do it, but David insisted he wanted to do it for himself.**

The first episode set the tone for old-fashioned knockabout comedy with David falling over chairs, getting soaked fully clothed in a Turkish bath, taking a nosedive over a settee and putting on a negligee without realising it. It led *Daily Mirror* TV writer Stan Sayer to declare, 'David is a modern Buster Keaton with most of that great silent film actor's gift of timing, rhythm and skill.'

Among Edgar's long-suffering colleagues who looked upon his unlikely achievements with amusement, alarm, incredulity and jealousy was Spencer, played by that fine actor Mark Eden, later to find infamy as the beast of Weatherfield, *Coronation Street's* Alan Bradley.

Mark remembers, 'David was brilliantly inventive and I knew then he was going to be a star. David was very popular with everyone and you could not fail to respond to his enthusiasm and his determination to make the show absolutely as good as possible.'

David Jason's flair for the physical side of being funny was given free rein in *Edgar Briggs* and he boldly grasped the challenge, insisting on doing all of his own stunts. Mark Eden said: 'Even when it involved big falls he insisted on doing it himself. He knew it would look better than using stunt men. Once we were on the top floor of one of those big old-fashioned houses in London near the Regent's Park canal. The script called for David and I to pretend to be window cleaners and he had to get out onto a window sill.

'As he got out he slipped and grabbed a rope and swung around a bit and then I had to grab him by this cardigan he was wearing but then he had to slip through the cardigan, which I was left holding, and crash several storeys to the ground. They were planning to use a stuntman for the final fall but David said, "No, no, I'll do it. It will look better," and of course he fell down into the pile of cardboard boxes quite brilliantly. But I wouldn't have dared to do it.

'He wanted to do everything himself. Another time we were in one of those crazy car chases and we had to go over a hump-backed bridge at high speed so

Opposite page:
David in the West
End farce *Look No
Hans!*

fast that the car took off. They had stunt drivers ready and waiting but David insisted he wanted to do it himself and he talked me into coming along for the most terrifying ride of my life. He kept saying it would be much better because the cameras would be able to capture our faces and our expressions of fear. The expression was genuine in my case as I smashed my head against the roof when we became airborne.'

All through his career David has been prepared to take the bumps and the bruises when called upon to turn in a very physical performance. But it was while he was making *The Odd Job Man* that he suffered a horrific accident which left his entire body seized up. 'I had to be thrown over a settee,' he recalls, 'and I ended up between the settee and a chair and landed on my head with the whole weight of my body on top of my head. I was trapped. I seized up so totally that I couldn't turn my head. I couldn't even get my arm up to scratch the back of my head. My arm wouldn't work and my hand wouldn't work either – I couldn't close my fingers into a fist.'

Much play was made of the fact that both these two beautiful very tall girls towered over David.

David was never one to shirk the chance of acrobatics to win a laugh when he was on stage and a new West End comedy *Look No Hans!* at the Strand Theatre proved the point.

Look No Hans! by John Chapman and Michael Pertwee was a farce set in West Berlin with David cast as a British car firm sales representative called Fisher who finds himself recruited by an industrial MI5. Lynda Bellingham played his wife whose arrival in Germany sets the cat among the dolly-birds Fisher has become acquainted with. They included a striking blonde Anita Graham as a put-upon stripper Mitzi, and Heather Alexander, an equally striking blonde beauty, as a fetching fraulein Heidi who spends much of the play in black boots and a backless maid's outfit. Much play was made of the fact that both these two beautiful, very tall girls towered over David.

David made the very most of every comic opportunity as filing cabinets banged him on the head or kicked him in the shins, safe doors threw him up in the air, and every ring of the doorbell or telephone sent him into frenzied scuttling around the stage.

Somewhat predictably, the critics did not much care for *Look No Hans!* when it opened on September 4, 1985. But almost to a man they were fulsome in their praise for David who gave his usual whole-hearted, energetic performance.

In his review for the *Daily Telegraph*, John Barber labelled David 'an athletic rubber-faced comic resembling a pug dog doing a fandango.' He added, 'There is not much to it beyond a comedian in a perpetual dither and a room full of doors and a half-undressed girl behind each.'

Irving Wardle in the *Times* praised David's 'marvellous unbroken chain of manic acrobatics.' and Milton Shulman in the London *Evening Standard* said: 'David Jason, who looks like a flyweight boxer but has the agility of an acrobatic dancer, is a natural comic. Without him I shudder to think what a quick oblivion would have awaited this rather tired farce.'

David's most glowing review came from Michael Coveney writing in the *Financial Times*. He said, 'David Jason played the compulsive joker rather like Dudley Moore on speed, and with technique. Jason's television popularity is no

David's ability to age up effectively led to
him also taking up the role of Blanco Webb
in Barker's wonderful prison comedy
series *Porridge*.

A publicity poster
for *White Cargo*.

BORDER FILM PRODUCTIONS (LONDON) LTD. *presents*
DAVID JASON   IMOGEN HASSALL *in* **WHITE CARGO** Cert
HUGH LLOYD   TIM BARRETT   EASTMAN COLOUR   **AA**

'His timing was so good, he was great
with props and he taught me the
visual importance of gags.'

flash in the pan. He's a genuinely funny actor, very fast and, like Groucho Marx, close to the nerve. Athletic too. I wish him luck when he finds a vehicle worthy of his talent.'

But work wasn't all knockabout comedy for David. He also played a 100-year-old gardener called Dithers in an early Ronnie Barker series called *Hark at Barker* and when Ronnie Barker moved across from ITV to the BBC and *Hark at Barker* turned into *His Lordship Entertains*, Ronnie was keen for old Dithers to make the move as well. The aged gardener was always popular and David's ability to age up effectively led to him also taking up the role of Blanco Webb in Barker's wonderful prison comedy series *Porridge*.

David starred in three memorable episodes: 'No Peace For The Wicked' and 'Happy Release' in 1975, and 'Pardon Me' in 1977. In 'No Peace For The Wicked', Fletch's attempts to find some some peace and quiet on a Saturday afternoon are scuppered by constant interruptions from prison officers and cons including a visit from Blanco proudly wheeling in a wooden mule it has taken him 15 years to make. Finally the chaplain enters and an exasperated Fletch throws him over the balcony so he can obtain solitary confinement.

'Happy Release' featured Fletch and Blanco in the prison infirmary together with a nasty piece of work called Norris who is in prison for just a few days. Norris cons Blanco out of all his worldly possessions – his wireless, his silver snuff box and a musical box – by cheating at Nine Card Brag. But Fletcher, using all his native cunning, hatches a plan to have Blanco retrieve all his valuables by giving his cellmate Godber a fake map of buried treasure – a hoard of £8,000 interred in Leeds. Knowing full well that Norris will obtain the map in exchange for Blanco's goods, Fletch has the added satisfaction of Norris being incarcerated for digging up the pitch at Leeds United.

'I have that poem framed in my house now, and it will always be one of my most prized posessions.'

In the brilliantly conceived episode 'Pardon Me', David left Slade Prison in comic style. Blanco had been inside for 17 years for the murder of his wife, a crime he had always sworn he did not commit. He felt so angry about his unjust incarceration that when offered parole he refused on the grounds that it amounted to an admission of guilt.

But after Fletch had successfully raised a petition for Blanco to be pardoned, Blanco was finally absolved of the blame for his wife's death and was granted the pardon and his freedom. He had protested all along that the killer was his wife's lover. During Blanco's final farewell to Fletch, the two men shook hands and Fletch urged Blanco to get even with the killer. 'Oh he died long ago,' said Blanco. 'I know. It were me that did it!'

Playing Blanco as a man twice his real age, David was almost unrecognisable with wisps of grey hair, spectacles and a doddery gait. Producer Sydney Lotterby recalls: 'It was quite remarkable how David could add on the years so convincingly. He was simply so talented and so dedicated. Everyone knew then that he was something special.

'Ronnie Barker was always known as "The Guvnor" because of his towering comedy talent. He really rated David's abilities highly so when we were looking around for a hapless nephew for the shop in Roy Clarke's *Open All Hours* we

Opposite page:
A big shot in *The Odd Job Man.*

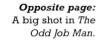

GRAND THEATRE, WOLVERHAMPTON
Managing Director & Licensee: Humphrey Stanbury   Box Office: 10 a.m. to 8 p.m.   (0902) 25244 5
Commencing **MONDAY, 24th MARCH, 1975 for one week**
Monday to Friday at 7.30 p.m.   Saturday at 5 & 8 p.m.   Matinee: Wednesday at 2.30 p.m.
PRICES: £1.30   £1.20   £1.10   £1.00   65p   50p

by arrangement with JOHN GALE (for Volcano Productions
PAUL ELLIOTT & DUNCAN C. WELDON
for TRIUMPH THEATRE PRODUCTIONS
present

DAVID JASON
(TOP SECRET LIFE OF EDGAR BRIGGS)

BOB GRANT
(ON THE BUSES)

DEREK NEWARK
(BARLOW)

ROSE HILL
('THINGAMMYBOB')

and

DOREEN KEOGH
('CONCEPTA' IN CORONATION ST.)

in

"DARLING MR. LONDON"

by

ANTHONY MARRIOTT
and BOB GRANT

with

VALERIE LEON
LEENA SKOOG JANET EDIS
VERONICA BARBIERI

Directed by
ANTHONY WILES

Designed by JOHN PAGE

A FORUM THEATRE, BILLINGHAM, PRODUCTION

David tops the bill in an early stage tour.

David is never happier than when he's involved in something practical – despite his fame he likes to do things himself!

naturally did not have to look very far. David was a delight.

'We filmed *Open All Hours* up in Doncaster where a hairdressing salon called Helen's Beautique became Arkwright's corner shop. David was always known as Little Feed because he used jokingly to grumble that he was only there to set up the laughs for Ronnie.

'But Granville became very popular in his own right thanks to Roy Clarke's marvellous writing and David's performances. My favourite memory is the night we had Granville recreating the famous "Singing in the Rain" number. David was so keen to get it right he must have spent hours getting it just so while providing a free cabaret for the good folk of Doncaster.'

Ronnie Barker thoroughly enjoyed the recordings as well. 'David Jason, Lynda Baron and I had great times on that series. We would be in Doncaster for three weeks doing the filmed sequences for two episodes each week. So work went on until midnight sometimes, with shouting, the noise of equipment and arc lights glaring. But nobody objected, though one chap did ask how long this would be going on for as he had to get up early for work!

'The BBC generally found an empty house for sale and that would have the canteen on the ground floor, David and myself sharing one bedroom as a dressing room and Lynda using the other. We'd put up posters and silly knick-knacks making it homelier, even though it was just for those three weeks.

On display in David's kitchen were little figurines of Charlie Chaplin, Buster Keaton and Laurel and Hardy.

'Our trio's rapport showed in the spirit of *Open All Hours*. We were three mates. On location you all get together at the end of the day, have dinner, crack open a bottle or two, relax and laugh. David Jason became a good friend. What a funny man. He and I have always had such rapport, ever since we first met at London Weekend Television in the half-hour comedy *The Odd Job Man*.

'What a wonderful sense of timing he has, with that marvellous rubber face. What a reliable and professional man to work with.'

For David Jason, Ronnie Barker was simply someone extra special. When Barker retired at the very height of his fame and popularity. David was one of the inner circle who knew all about the dramatic decision well in advance.

David says of Barker, 'He is basically an actor and the best comedy actor I have ever worked with. He was my hero, helpful, considerate, a wonderful teacher. I loved his generosity but I was more affected by his ability. So much so that I always used to call him "The Guvnor" behind his back.

'That was the word I used because there was no one better at his craft in the country. This was before *The Two Ronnies* and everything he did from then on reinforced my feelings. If Ronnie suffers from anything it's comic diarrhoea. He can't help being funny. Through the years I have seen more of Ronnie Barker than most people and I know he was a very great comedy actor, the best. I enjoyed working with him so much because it is always a pleasure to work at the top level. And he was always so quick.

'When he retired, he gave me something that I will always treasure. It is a poem, one of Ronnie's witty odes and at the end of it he says, "I now relinquish the honoured title of The Guvnor to my apprentice the boy Granville who is

entitled herewith to call himself The Guvnor." Although the nickname started as a joke it was always a secret mark of respect from me to Ronnie and to have him return it was just amazing. I have that poem framed in my house now and it will always be one of my most prized possessions.'

While *The Top Secret Life Of Edgar Briggs* was probably underrated, it nevertheless fell a very long way short of its objectives of turning David Jason into a household name. But producer Humphrey was convinced it was only a matter of time before David achieved a major breakthrough as a TV comedy star.

It duly came with *Lucky Feller*, a series about the eternal triangle – but with a difference. 'It was about this innocent little man Shorty Mepstead trying to run his little plumbing business with his elder brother Randy who was bedding Shorty's girlfriend,' says writer Terence Frisby. 'In the end, Randy got her pregnant and the younger brother, Shorty, had to marry her.'

David, naturally, had the role of Shorty, the gauche innocent who still lived at home in South East London with his mother and brother Randolph and believed he was the luckiest person in the world because he was surrounded by such ostensibly lovely people. Cheryl Hall, a bright, pretty and gifted 26-year-old actress, won the role of Kathleen, Shorty's girlfriend who gradually coaxes him out of his shyness. Peter Armitage, later to find fame in *Coronation Street*, was signed to play brother Randy.

Like so many of his co-stars, Cheryl took an instant liking to David and was immediately impressed by his flair for visual comedy and his meticulous approach to acting. 'He was so professional,' she reflects. 'His timing was so good, he was great with props and he taught me the importance of visual gags.

Above:
With Ian Richardson in *Porterhouse Blue*.

Opposite:
Athlete David takes to the track.

'Shorty was Mr Uncool, a man who never got anything right and we had a scene in a pub where he went to light my cigarette with his lighter. Being Shorty, of course, he activates the lighter and a huge flame shoots out and burns my entire nose. It was a tricky scene but David worked out all the angles perfectly and knew exactly where the camera should be so we could film the shooting flame then cut it so that my nose could be reddened for the next shot.

'David was always one hundred per cent committed. He lived, ate, and breathed acting and when he wasn't acting he was always talking about the business. He had that totally focussed approach and very much wanted to be a star.'

All looked extremely promising when it came to filming the first episode of *Lucky Feller*. One scene, in particular, at a Chinese restaurant had the studio audience in fits. 'I've never heard people laugh as much,' says writer Frisby. The scene involved Shorty taking girlfriend Kath out for a meal. The comic scenario had Shorty, hopelessly ignorant of Chinese cuisine, so drastically over-ordering from the menu that the waiter, played by Burt Kwouk, had to pull up another table to accomodate yet more plates piled with food.

As 1976 drew to a close, David could look back on a thoroughly satisfactory year.

Among the offerings were two dumplings which were to provide the audience with their cue for hysterical laughter – because Shorty had ordered prawn balls. Gazing at the spread with puzzled expression, Kath inquired, 'Which are the prawn balls?' Frisby recalls, 'The audience laughed like you've never heard. Then David pointed at the dumplings and said, "It must be those." Then Kath says, "Ooh, big aren't they?" and the audience laughed for another ten minutes so that David never managed to get out the pay-off line which was, "Well, they were kingsize prawns." We did umpteen takes and the audience were collapsing and David broke up before every take. Everyone laughed so much those three lines took half an hour to shoot.'

Lucky Feller was launched on September 2, 1976 and earned some plaudits from the TV critics. Sean Day-Lewis, writing in the *Daily Telegraph*, said, 'My response to David Jason as Shorty Mepstead is that he has a very characterful face and is more likeable than funny.' The *Stage*, assessing the new sit-com in the wake of *The Secret Life of Edgar Briggs*, remarked prophetically: 'Somewhere there is a writer whose ideas Mr. Jason can excecute to great effect but they have not met yet.'

At the end of the series Cheryl Hall presented David with a lovely charcoal drawing of Laurel and Hardy, two comedy heroes whom David much revered. She'd noticed that on display in David's kitchen were little figures of Charlie Chaplin, Buster Keaton, and Laurel and Hardy.

Almost immediately after filming finished on *Lucky Feller*, Cheryl and David went off on tour in the stage comedy *Darling Mr London* which opened at St. Anne's-on Sea on September 6, four days after *Lucky Feller* had hit the screen. As the tour progressed, *Darling Mr London* was able to cash in on the TV exposure which Cheryl and David were getting from *Lucky Feller* and it played to enthusiastic houses on its rounds of Southampton, Swansea, Wimbledon, Bradford and Bournemouth.

David played the central role of a hen-pecked international telephone operator called Edward Hawkins who has sought escapism in fantasy long-distance telephone affairs with a number of foreign 'call-girls'. But when the girls arrive in England for the Miss Europhone contest, they are determined to fit a face to the voice that has been charming them so consistently and they all descend at once on his home in West Drayton.

Chaos reigns. Behind the spare room door is Monique, the Parisian femme fatale anxious to show Edward the thrills of a French love affair, and behind another bedroom door is Sylvana who wants to make babies with Edward's help. Waiting in the wings equally ready to get down to their underwear are the Scandiavian sexpots Britt and Ingrid. A set which included six doors and French windows gave David plenty of scope to produce a fast-moving performance as he rushed from one to the other with the girls scampering across the stage in bikinis or their underwear.

All in all, *Darling Mr London* was an attractive package for anyone who liked to see television stars in person and pretty girls wearing precious little with plenty of laughs along the way. The play in general, and David in particular, garnered rave reviews.

The 'World Premiere' of *Darling Mr London*, as the *Stage* grandly announced it, was at the Billingham Forum on March 7, 1975, and the local critic Robert Brayshay of the *Evening Dispatch* said in his review, 'It must be one of the funniest plays to be presented there. The star of the show is David Jason whose natural gift for comedy gets boundless scope. He draws as much humour from physical actions as as from his lines and gives an exceptionally rewarding performance.'

Another columnist noted towards the end of the play's run, 'This amusing farce had some memorable moments especially when David Jason was on stage – which was most of the time.' At the Theatre Royal, Bath, *Darling Mr London* was given an equally warm welcome. *The Bristol Evening Post*'s critic Jeremy Brien labelled it 'one of the very best farces since the early Brian Rix offerings.' He wrote in his review that David was splendid in the central role and added: 'The evening is built around the talent of David Jason whose cueing in of the laughs, elaborate contortions, and brilliant command of the throw-away line, are at the heart of the entertainment.' Judith Boyd of *The Bath and West Evening Chronicle* found the comedy

A Sharp Intake of Breath swept surprisingly to No 1 in its first week and stayed there.

fast and furious and said: 'Most of the energy is burnt up by David Jason as Edward and his performance never loses any of its mind-boggling vigour.'

As 1976 drew to a close, David could look back on a thoroughly satisfactory year. Although *Lucky Feller* had not been a resounding hit, there were plans for another series of *Open All Hours* which had been well received by critics and public alike when it had quietly opened in February on BBC2.

While the BBC looked to build on the highly promising start of *Open All Hours*, David moved to Lew Grade's ATV at Elstree for yet another sitcom. It was called *A Sharp Intake of Breath* and it turned out to be a highly significant show in the TV career of David Jason because surprisingly it swept him for the first time to the top of the ratings, a position he has occupied many times since.

A Sharp Intake of Breath gave David the leading role of Peter Barnes, an ordinary man battling against the perils of officialdom in assorted shapes and sizes and trying to understand and beat 'the system'. Peter's belief in freedom of choice often involved an innocent third party getting dragged into his escapades. Regular cast members included Richard Wilson, now a household name as grumpy Victor Meldrew in *One Foot In The Grave*. David's brother Arthur was asked to appear as an engineer who called to mend a broken electric heater.

Launched on February 20, 1978, two years to the day after the launch of *Open All Hours*, *A Sharp Intake of Breath* swept surprisingly to number one in the ratings in its first week and stayed there.

David was understandably delighted. 'I've never had so many fan letters in my life,' he beamed. 'It's almost like being a pop star. I was confident about the series but I thought it would take a little time to get it right and that audiences would take a while to catch on. I think a theme of an ordinary bloke struggling against officialdom appealed right across the board.'

Just as it looked as though *A Sharp Intake of Breath* had finally elevated David Jason to stardom, the show was hit by tragedy when its creator and writer Ronnie Taylor died very suddenly from a mystery virus at the age of 57. David was desperately upset. Not only had Ronnie become a good friend but together they had worked hard to build up the character of Peter Barnes as the little man always falling foul of bureaucracy. It had been a fruitful and harmonious partnership.

He had started late on the ladder to success, but now he had achieved it.

It seemed that the death of Ronnie Taylor was to be the end of the success story for *A Sharp Intake of Breath* but David and producer-director Stuart Allen were determined to save the show. But another writer was needed.

By good fortune, David happened to meet comedy writer Vince Powell on an episode of the TV charades show *Give Us A Clue*. 'I suddenly realised we had the same sense of humour,' said David, 'and I persuaded him to have a go at writing *A Sharp Intake of Breath*.'

A further three series were made including one episode where David appeared with an eye-patch because of a bad attack of conjunctivitis. Throughout, David won Allen's admiration for his comedic flair. 'I always thought David Jason was immensely clever and immensely funny,' he says. 'He was such a worker, so keen on all the detail. Everything that I admired about an artist and a performer David had, and more talent and drive than anyone I've met before or since.

'He was dedicated to his work and immensely creative with his comedy. So much so that he would get a laugh where I never could have believed there was a laugh to be had. He was superb.'

A Sharp Intake of Breath had finally taken David to the top. He had started late on the ladder to success but, now he had achieved it, little did he know what was to come. Another comedy show, *Only Fools and Horses*, was to turn him into Britain's most popular TV actor, and a coveted Best Actor award from the British Academy of Film and Television Arts (BAFTA) awaited him further down the line for his brilliant portrayal of irascible 64-year-old Cambridge university porter Skullion in *Porterhouse Blue*. That proved to David's peers that he was a fine straight actor. 'That was the greatest accolade I've managed to receive,' said David. 'It put me into a different category from "That's the bloke who can only do Cockney voices."'

Opposite:
David in one of the saucier scenes from *White Cargo.*

CHAPTER FOUR

The Darling Buds of May

*I*n the Spring of 1991 Britain was in the grip of a recession and for many life was nothing less than grim. The nation was in desperate need of cheering up and, as if on cue, David Jason stepped forward to provide it.

From the moment he appeared on ITV screens as happy-go-lucky, lovable Pop Larkin in *The Darling Buds of May*, David warmed the hearts of the nation in the most extraordinary way. A staggering 17 million viewers tuned in to the first episode of the series based on the books by HE Bates about a close-knit family living in the Kent countryside in the 1950s and that huge audience was enough to take the series straight to the top of the TV ratings. And there it stayed.

Quite simply, everybody fell in love with Pop Larkin and his delightful family. They revelled in the way the Larkins loved the simple things in life like spending hours eating together, they loved their family joy, their laughter, their spirit and their generosity to all those whom the Larkins so readily welcomed into their home set deep among the hop fields, orchards and fields of the county known as the garden of England.

A staggering 17 million viewers turned on for the first episode of the series based on the books by HE Bates.

Naturally David, now sporting mutton chops as Pop Larkin, largely carried the show but he was given terrific support from Pam Ferris as Ma Larkin and, notably, from a beautiful newcomer called Catherine Zeta Jones as their gorgeous daughter Mariette. Catherine has now gone on to major Hollywood stardom.

For David Jason the most important aspect of the stunning success of *The Darling Buds of May* was not just the way Yorkshire Television's glossy adaptation of the HE Bates novels was such a ratings success. The unprecedented audience bonanza, the international sales and the videos which followed were all pleasing enough but definitely secondary to David's main reaction.

'I was overwhelmed and enormously heartened that such a simple family story with no sex, no violence and no bad language could attract more viewers

Opposite page: David and Catherine Zeta Jones share an intimate moment.

Above:
The cast of *The Darling Buds of May.*

Opposite page:
Pop Larkin.

than all those dreadful action adventures of the time like *The A Team* or *Miami Vice* where people get blown away in just about every scene,' said David.

'Of course when Vernon Lawrence at Yorkshire TV sent me the HE Bates books and approached me about the idea I realised straight away that it could make a marvellous nostalgic series set in the 1950s, a time of almost total innocence. I knew Pop Larkin was potentially a great character to play, and I also knew, in spite of what people might think, that he could be completely different from Del-Boy.

'I also knew, in spite of what people might think, that he could be completely different from Del Boy.'

'*The Darling Buds of May* also appealed to me because it seemed to be the kind of television that is hardly seen any more. A series about a whole wonderful fictional family that whole real-life families could sit and enjoy together without any fear of embarrassment. Wholesome fun seems to have become sadly a little unfashionable these days and *Darling Buds* seemed to be doing something to reverse that trend.

'What stunned me was the response. Every episode going out as the most popular programme of the week ahead of *Coronation Street* and *EastEnders*, was unbelievable. The Larkins are actually all pretty nice people being on the whole jolly decent to each other. The books were lovely and charming and happily I think we managed to capture much of that naive and lyrical appeal on the screen.

'A lot of the fans of *Darling Buds* seemed to be young people, which both delighted and surprised me. I always knew teenagers identified with Del but I got so many kids yelling "Hey, Perfick!" at me and enthusing about Pop Larkin that I knew *Darling Buds* had clicked with them too.'

Vernon Lawrence, the Yorkshire TV boss who co-produced *Darling Buds of May* with Richard Bates, the nephew of HE Bates, must take much of the credit for David being cast as Pop Larkin because Richard originally wanted Bob Hoskins to be the star.

But just at the time *The Darling Buds of May* project was gathering momentum, Hoskins was riding high as a film star in movies like *The Cotton Club* and *Who Killed Roger Rabbit?* In principle, Vernon Lawrence had nothing against Hoskins. He felt he would make a fine Pop Larkin. But with a flourishing film career and big movie offers coming in, Hoskins was thought unlikely to give Yorkshire TV more than one series.

Vernon felt David Jason was ideal for Pop Larkin. He emphasised to Richard Bates that David had attributes which Hoskins did not have. David had a lovable quality while Hoskins' image had been built on tough gangster roles.

It took Vernon five weeks but finally he brought Richard Bates round to his way of thinking. David took only ten days before making up his mind to play Pop Larkin. *Darling Buds of May* was launched on British Television on April 5, 1991, and the 17 million viewers who switched on enjoyed every moment.

'It had nostalgia, something we all love,' said Vernon. 'It is wonderfully English. Better still it's rural English. It's about a family who live the way we secretly all love to live, never paying the income tax, never bothering about modern fads like dieting.

'It's about a little man who pits himself against bureaucracy and

David's remarkable popular appeal certainly transformed a promising idea into a surefire hit.

wins, and who breaks through all the class barriers of the period – he deals in junk, but hobnobs with brigadiers and the lord of the manor. It's good clean fun. And it's got that very, very important ingredient, a genuine star – David Jason.'

David's remarkable popular appeal certainly transformed a promising idea into a surefire hit. And he threw himself enthusiastically into the production with his usual professionalism and chirpy good humour. He chose a typically individual way of establishing a good relationship with ample actress Pam Ferris who played Ma Larkin. Pam added two stone to her size 14 figure by packing in the pasta but even then had to wear masses of rubber padding to fill the role of 16-stone Ma Larkin.

David knew that one of their early scenes was troubling Pam, and considering the two of them were scheduled to spend an afternoon splashing about in the bath together while eating a huge fry-up, he could quite understand

Opposite page:
Enjoying all the
good things in life
as Pop Larkin.

Boy but that means they don't realise Del-Boy is a brilliant artistic creation of his. In *Darling Buds* people believe Pop Larkin is him. He is a very talented actor and great fun to work with. The first time I met him I gave him a peck on the cheek and said: "That's the first of many."'

Pam and David both found that they piled on the pounds as life with the Larkins revolved very much round eating. David packed on an extra one and a half stone and went on a diet while Pam expanded up to 14 stone. She said: 'The Larkins are such powerful characters. They're so pro-life. They're into giving, loving, making love, eating and being generous – with themselves. And they spend so much time eating. They start the day with a huge breakfast, then there's a mid-morning sandwich snack, a proper cooked lunch, high tea of ham off the bone or kippers, followed by a full hot supper, finished of with cocktails.

Pam and David both found they piled on the pounds, as life with the Larkins revolved very much around eating.

'We both ate so much while filming. We couldn't cheat with just a tiny scrap of food on the end of a fork, we had to shovel it in just like the Larkins. Once we did a scene where David and I were eating chocolate and pickled onions in bed. Then, on yet another day, we re-shot the same scene eating kippers. I never want to see another kipper in my life. And that scene was eventually cut!'

Pop and Ma Larkin certainly captured the affection of the nation. When the video version of the series was rushed into the shops it sold £1 millon worth of copies in the first four days and HE Bates's classic novels staged a sudden revival in sales. The truth of their relationship of course was that although they lived so happily together with their huge family they were never actually married. Although he was blissfully content with his Ma, Pop somehow never quite managed to make it official.

This cheerfully unmarried condition mirrored David's happy and long established real-life relationship with Myfanwy Talog, the attractive Welsh actress who shared his life until her sad death from cancer at the age of 49 in March 1995, made all the more tragic because twice Myfanwy thought she had beaten the disease.

Born in Caerwys, Clwyd, daughter of a school attendance officer and a bus conductor, Myfanwy's career began in the late 1960s and was really launched with the huge success of Ryan and Ronnie, a comedy double act on Welsh and English television in the early 1970s.

After that, Myfanwy appeared in many of the long-running Welsh television series of the 1970s and 1980s and in the latter half of the Eighties she became a national institution in S4C's soap opera *Dinas* in which she played Cynthia Doyle, a characteristically salt-of-the earth Welsh woman.

Myfanwy was well established in the BBC Wales studios when she and David first met when David was on tour in a play in South Wales in the mid 1970s. He was immediately smitten by Myfanwy's striking blue eyes, natural red hair, handsome appearance and sense of fun and thereafter she and David remained very close.

Myfanwy was credited by David's friends for the tasteful decoration which transformed the stylish country home set in an acre of land which the couple shared in Wendover, near Aylesbury. Friends felt she could have had a second

Opposite page:
David with his
beloved Myfanwy.

career as an interior decorator and at home with David she was always a vivacious hostess. Although Myfanwy worked a lot in her native Wales and David's work commitments meant he was frequently away from home, they were as close to being married as it is possible to be without the certificate.

Certainly Myfanwy was a great favourite with David's mother, Olwen, who often referred to her as the 'daughter-in-law'. Olwen was especially pleased her youngest son had fallen for a Welsh girl and Olwen made it clear she would have been very happy if Myfanwy had become David's wife.

David and Myfanwy frequently visited his mother who, until her death, still lived in a humble council flat not far from the Lodge Lane home which was demolished to make room for a car park some 25 years ago. David had suggested a home in the country for his mother in her twilight years but she was fiercely independent and preferred to stay near her old friends.

As a young actor, David once said in an interview that marriage was like 'throwing yourself in the river when you only want a drink.' But as his relationship with Myfanwy continued to blossom he said, 'That was a flip remark that has come back to haunt me. I really am not against marriage but I'm fine as I am. Call us constant companions. We are very happy with the way things are. We are both busy so we do not see that much of each other, but that suits us fine. This arrangement works for us. It's nice, it's refreshing. It means that when we

David takes a ride in the famous Larkin motor.

get together we have got things to talk about. It's something to look forward to.'

David was happy to declare publicly that Myfanwy was 'the great love of my life' and there is no doubt that the press tag for Myfanwy of 'constant companion' did no justice to the love, devotion and stability she provided for David in his acting career.

David was always happy to declare publicly that 'Myfanwy was the great love of my life.'

David, for his part, gave Myfanwy unstinting support in 'the great fight' as she called her battle against cancer which began when she discovered a lump in her breast while on holiday abroad in 1990. 'My initial thought was, "This is the end,"' she said.

Myfanwy was warned that a malignant growth, which she and David nicknamed 'The Alien', could mean her losing her breast. David insisted on being with her when she went into hospital for exploratory surgery. Myfanwy recalled, 'We told the surgeon: "We trust you utterly. Just do what you have to do."' The tumour was removed and her breast saved and three years later Myfanwy was back on stage and, she said, 'feeling fantastic.' But the disease was to take a fatal grip.

Throughout her five-year fight against the disease, Myfanwy worked alongside charities, talking about her illness and trying to remove some of the stigma surrounding it. After undergoing surgery and radiotherapy, Myfanwy later spoke of her ordeal and how it had brought her even closer to David. 'We faced everything together right from when I first found out,' she said. 'It improved our relationship and it strengthened what we had between us.'

David frequently broke away from filming commitments to be with Myfanwy and hold her hand as she was wheeled in for treatment. 'David has been a tower of strength,' she said at a time when she thought her cancer was in remission. 'I cannot stress enough how important it is to have the support of loved ones. David made all the difference.'

Myfanwy ultimately lost her brave five-year battle but not before she had been able to enjoy moving into a splendid new home with David and sharing one of the proudest moments of David's life when he was awarded the OBE.

They were on holiday together in Florida and David was itching to share his OBE secret with Myfanwy. On the day he knew his OBE would become official back in England, he and Myfanwy were having lunch with friends and he wrote out his new address on a card and gave it to Myfanwy to pass across the table to their friends. David remembers, 'As she glanced at it, I took it back from her and said, "Hang on a minute, there's something missing." That's when I wrote the initials OBE after my name and handed it back to her. She did a double-take. She was absolutely stunned.' Then the penny dropped and Myfanwy flung her arms round David and whooped for joy.

David says, 'After all the euphoria I got up from the table to phone my mum to ask if she had heard the news. And can you believe what she said, "Yes I have. I suppose it'll cost me money for me to speak to you now. What I want to know is when are you coming round to mend my cooker?" I was phoning from the other side of the world about my OBE and all Mum wanted to know was when I was going to fix her cooker! Actually it was wonderful because it brought me straight back down to earth.'

CHAPTER FIVE

Only Fools & Horses

*T*he best-loved show on British television began life as just the germ of an idea in the ever-fertile mind of top comedy writer John Sullivan. He is the quietly spoken genius who was so determined to make it as a television writer he got himself a job as a scene shifter at the BBC in order to get his scripts seen by the right people.

Back in the late 1970s David Jason was just another highly regarded comedy actor. He was best known for his superb slapstick abilities in ITV shows like *A Sharp Intake of Breath* and as perky shopworker Granville, the comic feed to Ronnie Barker in the BBC's *Open All Hours*. But the link-up of David Jason's award-winning acting and John Sullivan's brilliant writing was to be one of those partnerships that make television history.

Sullivan openly admits that he sat down to write *Only Fools and Horses* for one reason. 'I wrote the pilot out of a desperate need to get some money,' he declared. His first hit, *Citizen Smith*, had run its course and other comedy concepts bit the dust before Sullivan broached the idea of *Readies*, as *Only Fools and Horses* was first known. It was a lively streetwise series set in colourful multi-racial London where the language could be fruity and there was always a gritty realistic struggle to survive going on just underneath the laughs. At first his BBC superiors were frightened off by the uncompromising content. Life with the Trotters was anything but cosy.

Only Fools and Horses had been born from a conversation Sullivan had one night with TV producer Ray Butt in the BBC club. The two men had worked together on *Citizen Smith* and now they were relaxing over a drink and talking about their origins and their childhoods. Butt's parents, it transpired, had a stall on Roman Road market and Butt had himself worked on street markets as a kid. Sullivan had also worked in the market when he was at school.

'We started talking about the various characters,' Sullivan remembers, 'and we both finally agreed that the most interesting people were the fly-pitchers with their suitcases and total disregard for licences. They would turn up sometimes for an hour, sometimes for ten minutes, and then they would be away on their toes. They were always funny characters, always selling absolute rubbish like mock perfume.'

Over the next few weeks Sullivan and Butt would meet up at Butt's local, The Three Kings on the corner of London's North End Road and Talgarth Road, and sit talking until gradually Sullivan began forming the idea of a family with two brothers separated by a large age gap. Sullivan envisaged a fraternal relationship where one brother was a man and the other was a little kid so that the relationship was one that was protective. The idea of an arms-round-the-shoulder fraternal love fascinated Sullivan.

From there Sullivan began weaving in various characteristics. Crucially he decided that Rodney, the younger brother, should be earnest and artistic and would not enjoy the life that elder brother Del lived. And yet he simply had to be tolerant of brother Del's ways. He had no choice in the matter because that was where the money was coming from. 'I was using real people and real situations from my own life. And to represent the older generation there would be this wonderful Granddad, grumpy but loveable,' says Sullivan.

Finally Sullivan sent Butt a script. 'It was marvellous,' Butt remembers. 'Simple as that.' Bursting with enthusiasm Butt took the script to inspirational BBC comedy boss John Howard Davies, the man behind classics like *The Good Life* and *Fawlty Towers*. This time, to Butt's joy, the response was more than encouraging. There would be no pilot, but there would be a series.

Butt and Sullivan were elated but casting proved to be a problem. Nicholas Lyndhurst was the first to be signed up to play Rodney. He had enjoyed great success as teenager Adam going through growing pains in another BBC sit-com *Butterflies* and both John Howard Davies and Butt agreed he was an excellent choice. Next to be cast was Lennard Pearce as Granddad. 'It was that lovely voice of his,' says Sullivan. 'It was a deep, croaky voice, a great voice. As soon as Lennard left the audition I said, "That's him!"'

The biggest problem now remained. Who could they get to play the key role of Derek Trotter? Butt and Sullivan racked their brains but no obvious names presented themselves. First choice for the role of Del Boy was Enn Reitel, who with his long face bore more than a passing resemblance to Nicholas Lyndhurst. They could certainly have passed as brothers. But he was not available.

Jim Broadbent was the next actor to be offered the part. But he had just opened in a play at Hampstead and it was transferring to the West End. A fine, conscientious actor, Broadbent felt he would be unable to give all his energy to the play if he was doing a TV series as well. Ray Butt could only admire him for his honesty and later used him in another role in *Only Fools and Horses* as the loathsome policeman Roy Slater.

Continuing his search, Butt went to look at an actor appearing in a play called *Moving* with Penelope Keith. He didn't find his Del but he did find another important member of the *Only Fools and Horses* cast – Roger Lloyd Pack who plays Trigger. The moment Lloyd Pack walked on stage Butt was immediately struck by his likeness to Sullivan's description of Trigger. In the very first episode the explanation is given for Trigger's name. Is it because he packs a gun? No, it's because he looks like a horse.

The link-up of David Jason's award-winning acting and John Sullivan's brilliant writing was to be one of the partnerships that made TV history.

Opposite page: David with his coveted BAFTA award.

By now filming dates were being firmed up for *Only Fools and Horses*, deadlines were approaching, and Butt concedes: 'I was stuck.' The whole course of David Jason's career was changed when Butt, still racking his brains for the right Del Boy, sat down one night to watch a repeat of *Open All Hours*. He saw a scene where David had something of a solo performance as Granville the ageing errand boy clowning around in the back store of the old shop. Suddenly the solution to his problem was obvious.

Next day Butt went into the office and rang Sullivan and put forward his idea of David Jason for Del Boy. But Sullivan was not happy at all. He could not see David in the role and when Butt then went to his bosses, they were not keen on the idea either precisely because of David's strong connection with *Open All Hours*.

As creator of the character of Del Boy, Sullivan felt genuine misgivings about David Jason taking on the role. 'I'd only seen him in *A Sharp Intake of Breath*,' he reasoned, 'and that was all very slapstick, falling over on the floor, opening the washing machine and all the water coming out. I thought that was his style and I was saying that Del had to be sharp, very sharp, tough, an aggressive little guy who has lived in the streets and survived.'

David later recalled: 'John couldn't believe it because I'd played this dopey, wonderful, lovable, Northern character Granville and thought there was no way I could play this brash, up-front, smart, fast-talking, fast-thinking South Londoner. John was not impressed at all. I will always be indebted to Ray. He stuck to his guns.'

David with his
A Bit of a Do co-
star Gwen Taylor.

Butt staunchly refused to take no for an answer. He was convinced that David would fill Del's shoes admirably and he wasn't going to give up that easily. Finally Butt sent David a script after winning an agreement from everyone on the production that David should at least be allowed to come in and read with Nick Lyndhurst.

David could hardly believe his eyes when the script arrived. He found himself laughing out loud and having to pause for breath.'I couldn't wait to turn to the next page,' he remembers. 'It was one of the best scripts I'd ever read to that point – and certainly the best characters.'

Although the script leaped off the page at David, astonishingly he was unclear which role was being earmarked for him. 'Apart from playing Granville, I'd played old men,' he explains. 'I didn't obviously think they wanted me to play Granddad but the thought struck me because I had always been playing silly old characters. I'd worked with Ronnie Barker as his 100-year-old gardener Dithers and played an old man in *Porridge*. I thought Ray might want me to play Granddad. There was no reason I should naturally be the right casting for someone nearer my own age because that had never happened to me. But when he said: what part do you think you'd be right for, I immediately said: 'Del Boy. He's a great character.'

Sullivan remembers the read-through vividly. 'They had a little read and although they'd never met before, it was immediate – just like you see it now. They both went into their characters. It was incredible. They had this wonderful chemistry. David was perfect all along and I didn't realise just how perfect he was for the part.' In fact, David and Nicholas did not know each other although they had previously met briefly some three years before when Nicholas was working on a kids programme for London Weekend Television called *Our Show*. Nicholas had actually interviewed David about his series *Lucky Feller*.

Crucially he decided that Rodney, the younger brother, should be earnest and artistic and would not enjoy the life that elder brother Del lived.

After just five minutes of David and Nicholas reading together, Butt and John Sullivan grinned at each other, nodded, and agreed: 'We've got our Del and Rodney.' And Lennard revelled from the start in Granddad's idleness. When Del described him in episode one as 'the out of work lamplighter waiting for gas to make a comeback,' he had trouble containing his own laughter.

Now Sullivan had come round to his way of thinking, Butt set about winning the approval of his BBC bosses. They were worried David had been over-exposed from *Open All Hours* and was too well established in the role of Granville. Butt could understand their reservations but said he could not agree. He stressed that David would be so very different as Del Boy. 'I knew David could do it,' he says. 'He was just absolutely right – and still is right.'

'They tried to dissuade Ray,' David recalls. 'The hierarchy said, no, that's not a good idea. They said they don't even look like brothers. Ray said: "That's the fun of it!"'

Sullivan, his blind spot about David suddenly brushed away, was especially

pleased that David Jason and Nicholas Lyndhurst looked so very different. Nicholas was just 19 years old when the first episode was filmed and he was tall, very slim, and gangling whereas David was small by comparison and squat.

Sullivan had indicated in the scripts that he wanted the younger brother to be tall and the elder not so. Thinking ahead, Sullivan wanted them to look different to lay the doubt about whether they shared the same parentage. He also wanted to make it look as though they were the only two people in the world who believed they were brothers. Having sown the seeds of doubt from the very start, Sullivan was able to make great capital out of and exploit the suspicion in years to come.

What was beyond question was David's own belief that he could be Del Boy once he had read the script. 'I knew I could do it. I was convinced. And at the final reading they said to Nick, Lennard and me: "We are going with you three!"'

Lyndhurst knew straight away that the new threesome would work. 'A lot of people upstairs at the BBC did not believe David and I could play brothers. We look so different and we have completely different styles. But as soon as we started reading the scripts together it was obvious there was a chemistry between the two of us and with Lennard as well,' he said.

'We struck up an instant friendship that has lasted ever since. We are never at a loss for what to say to each other. We can talk about anything. We have completely different ways of switching off, of becoming totally detached from work when we want to be. He hand-builds vintage motorcycles and is brilliant with anything mechanical. I love the outdoor stuff – like watersports and flying. But most important we just have tremendous respect for each other.

'When I read a script I know how he is going to play a scene and say a line

The Trotter brothers enjoy a cocktail beneath the palm trees.

and I'm sure he knows in advance how I'm going to play my lines. So there are no big surprises when we get together. We just get on terribly well.'

Remarkably, even at that earliest stage, David was acutely aware that *Only Fools and Horses* was something very special, not just another comedy series. 'I remember going to the bar with Nick and Lennard and I remember I said: "This is not an ordinary sit-com. This is not sit-com, it's more drama. There's an unknown title for this. Everyone calls it sit-com but what John Sullivan has done has superseded that." I sensed it.'

The very first episode, 'Big Brother', went out on September 8, 1981. And even in the opening scene, with Rodney and Granddad arguing over the pronunciation of Sidney Poitier's name the relationship of the characters was revealed as Del came bustling in, glanced at the television, and said, 'Personally I pronounce it Harry Belafonte, but you two please yourselves.' A young, energetic and distinctly slimline Jason was just brilliant as Del. He gazed into the mirror and said, 'S'il vous plait, s'il vous plait. What an enigma. I get better looking every day. Can't wait for tomorrow.'

Jason was so alive, so energetic, so full of chat as Del he was simply irresistible. John Sullivan set out his stall straight away. Rodney's resentment at Del's dominance was right there at the very beginning. Del found Rodney doing his 'accounts' to try to keep a track of the figures behind the widely differing incomes. But as so often afterwards Del just blew his protests away in a blast of hilarious patter.

When he hears of the figures actually being written down Del pauses with alarm, with his sharp Austin Reed jacket only half on. 'Well Granddad there you are. A lot of people told me what a right dipstick I was to make my brother a partner in the business. And this only goes to prove how bloody right they were. You dozy little twonk, Rodney. This is prima facie evidence. The taxman gets hold of that and he'll put us away for three years.'

Del is hilariously appalled that Rodney could even consider he is a cheat, which of course even at this very early stage he quite obviously is. Jason is twinkling on all cylinders as he continues, jacket still only half-on. 'Cheating you?! Cheating?! You?! What's that rumbling noise?'

'I can't hear nothing,' replies Rodney, guilelessly taking the bait.

'Oh, it's all right,' says Del. 'It's only mum turning in her grave.'

And he follows up with a full frontal attack on Rodney for having the total lack of consideration to be born a full 13 years after he was. Jacket at last shrugged into place, he says, 'You have been nothing but an embarrassment to me since the day you was born. You couldn't be like any other little brother, could you? And come along a couple of years after me. Oh no, you had to wait 13 years so while all the other mods were having punch-ups down at Southend and going to the Who concerts, I was at home baby-sitting. I could never get your oyster milk stains out of me Ben Shermans. I used to finds rusks in me Hush Puppies.'

David Jason looked to be thoroughly enjoying himself as he revelled in Del's deliciously rich dialogue. 'Mum was 39 when she fell for you. Did you know that for the first three months of her pregnancy you was treated as an ulcer. And to this day I sometimes think the original diagnosis was correct.'

David Jason knew then he was on a winner. 'There was more weight in the characters, they were so much more full-blooded and three-dimensional than anything I had played before. Because it was so well written we could go against the normal theme of things and try and make the characters more funny. I discovered when I read the script that it was so well written and the characters were so good that you could really concentrate on the other side of it and let the characters and dialogue work for you. I love all the sides to Del. He can be really clever and manipulative but he's got a heart of gold. Del is a tragi-comic figure, trapped by his background, his environment and by himself. Yet he's an eternal optimist, a rubber ball who has the ability to bounce back no matter how badly life lets him down.

'Since that time, that's what we've done. You didn't have to invest very much in it. We do know that the characters can be very funny, very silly, emotional and moving. So it was a great mixture and having accepted that was the way to play it, touch wood it's worked.

'The writing is so good that *Only Fools and Horses* does not require so much effort from me. Del was once selling lace handkerchiefs and shouting, "Made in France at Chantilly. But due to a printer's error the labels came out Made in Taiwan, so we can offer them to selected customers cheap." They are such fine scripts I don't interfere. In the early days I used to encourage John to push the characters a bit further because I could see inside his writing that he was worth much more than making jokes. John is not just a joke writer, he is much more than that. He is a fine writer about people and relationships with real observations to make about life.

'The way he makes them work so beautifully is to have the family interact. Right at the beginning we had this episode where Del finds some lead on a building site and it turns out to be an atomic air raid shelter. Rodney then convinces Del that we should rebuild this shelter on top of the flats and as an experiment they spend a weekend inside.

'Of course Rodney takes it seriously and goes and gets all the batteries and so on while Del comes in his silk pyjamas with his name on the top. Then there was Granddad who was the only one of us who had really been through a war of course. The brilliance of Sullivan was that he was able to trap these three guys in a room for over half an episode. The only people who had done that before were *Steptoe and Son*, again thanks to tremendous writing.

'But what Sullivan managed to do when we were all trapped inside this shelter busy taking the mickey out of each other but mainly Granddad was wonderful. Rodney said, "It doesn't matter Granddad because in the next war we will be all right because we will be in this lead-lined shelter. We might be in here for two or three weeks." Granddad says, "Well what happens after we get out, there won't be anything." Del says, "There'll always be a little Paki shop open somewhere."

'But then after the joke the mood changes when Granddad becomes thoughtful and says, "Yeah, that's what they said during the last War. They said they would make homes fit for heroes. All they did was make heroes fit for homes." And suddenly this old boy who we have been busy taking the mickey out of has said something profound and moving that reaches out to all generations. That got to both Rodney and Del. And to me and Nick.

'I think it was at that moment that I realised that John Sullivan had got so much more inside him than an ordinary comedy writer. Not only were his scripts very funny, full of funny characters saying lots of funny lines but he was also able to move people, to get them emotionally involved. There was real weight there. Once we'd done the first series and John Sullivan had seen the characters come to life as we portrayed them, it gave him the spur and he could see the way we were going and could write them from great strength. The guy is a genius.'

At first the viewing public could hardly have agreed less. Although David, Ray Butt and John Sullivan all had high hopes for *Only Fools and Horses*, the first series did only moderately well. 'I think only about 12 people saw it and three of them were my family,' laughs Sullivan. He can afford to laugh now but at the time Sullivan was desperately disappointed as both he and Butt believed so strongly in the show.

Neither John Sullivan nor Ray Butt was confident that a second series would be commissioned. They simply held their breath. Finally they heard that the BBC was prepared to risk a second series thus following the long-held BBC tradition of allowing a show to have 'the right to fail'.

The first series did not merit a repeat and the second series also failed to make a significant impact in the ratings. But to the joy of Sullivan, David and everyone who had worked so hard on the show, repeats of the second series suddenly took *Only Fools and Horses* high into the Top Ten TV ratings. *Only Fools and Horses* was born. By the end of the third series, *Only Fools and Horses* was pulling in 15 million viewers and it has proved to be a massive ratings winner ever since.

'The initial reaction was very disappointing,' said David. 'It was only during the third series that people really started tuning in. I was amazed by the reaction when it arrived. Wherever I went people recognised me. I got mobbed in shops. At first I thought, "It's fantastic, like being a pop star." I had been in the business for 18 years and for about 12 of those years I was completely in the wilderness. That was how I expected the rest of my life to be – just fooling about on the end of some pier.

'I was really poor. I must have played every major town in this country and stayed in some of the worst digs imaginable and got up to some tricks to survive that would surprise even Del. One of my dodges was to be the last down to breakfast and then to hoover up absolutely everything. Sometimes you would be lucky, but sometimes it would be a minute piece of toast and a thin rasher of bacon. Then you had to try to make that last all day until just before the show when you had a sandwich. And after the show, maybe a couple of beers and a bag of chips on the way home. We had to manage on no money at all because we spent it all on Thursday nights after pay chasing women!

'I really like playing Del because he sometimes gets the girl. When you're a character actor you rarely get to kiss the girls. It's the leading men who get the passionate bedroom scenes. But Del has love scenes too! He just has a lot more front than I have. Del is all mouth and trousers and will go up to a girl and say "Hello darlin."' I would never do that.

'Del is wonderful to play because he is such a gentle person underneath all the brash bravado. He has that sensational sense of humour and at the same time he is sympathetic to those who are down. He will give a couple of extra apples to an old girl but if he sees someone who can afford it he will rob them instead.

The biggest problem remained. Who could they get to play the key role of Derek Trotter?

'The public seem to love him. I've had more free rides in taxis since Del came on the scene than I can remember. I always felt a special affinity, I know the world that Del comes from and sometimes I even try to offer an occasional line to John Sullivan. Once in Brighton market when I was out with my brother I heard a stallholder telling his customers to come a bit closer. He said, "At these prices I can't afford to deliver." There is a lot of wonderful wit out there and John Sullivan's great skill is that he constantly taps into it.'

Although it was essentially a three-man show, there was no doubting that David as Del Boy was the star. There was something incredibly infectious about his optimism and his constant promise to Rodney that this time next year they would be millionaires. The public warmed to Del's wheeling and dealing, his tremendous energy, and the fact that he was always up to something somewhere yet never really did anyone any harm.

The audience quickly cottoned on that Del would take a quid off anyone but he would never hit them over the head. And if someone was in trouble he would be the first to try to help out. He had brought up Rodney and he respected old people which was why he looked after first Granddad and then Uncle Albert. He was the type to walk round the estate at Christmas to make sure the old folk were all right and would know where there were some Christmas puddings going a bit cheap. Del clearly cared for people. He might have a rough exterior but if you were in trouble Del would help you out. It was the old working class ethic: I don't have anything but half of what I have is yours – if you need it. David has always been quick to give Sullivan great credit for his Del Boy creation and his superb scripts. But David's own contribution to the characterisation of Derek Trotter must not be underestimated.

Presented by Sullivan with the initial outline of Del, David was able to add his own stamp to the character by drawing on his memories of a builder called Derek Hockley whom he once worked for in East London during his days as an electrician.

David recalled, 'Del was described by John Sullivan in the outline of his stage notes and I thought, "That reminds me of Derek – the rings and the gold." As I was reading it, I thought this is more and more like this guy. Then when we came to the camel-hair coat – Derek always wore one.

'John at that time imagined Del to be pot-bellied, a beer gut, and long hair. It was at a time when hair was very thick and full. Again, I said he should have short hair. The directors did not see him like that but Derek Hockley always had hair which was dead smart, neatly parted, and had that swagger.'

Kitting out Del was a real labour of love for the BBC costume department, but as you might imagine the jewellery was not quite as genuine as it might have been. The half-sovereign rings are definitely fake and usually replaced after each series because they're so cheap the gold paint wears off. They come from cheap stores in London's Soho and cost only a few pence. But Del's necklace with the huge 'D' on is not so cheap. Costume designer Robin Stubbs had it specially made for around £70. The camel-hair coats once came from a shop near the BBC Television Centre in Shepherd's Bush, London but it closed down and now the buyers have to venture into the West End. Del's flashier suits came from Austin Reed in Regent Street at around £200 a time. Stubbs said: 'We have to be discreet when we go in for them. If David is recognised he is mobbed.' The ties came from Tie-Rack, his raincoat came from Dickens and Jones in Regent Street and his shirts from Austin Reed and Marks and Spencer.

Next day, Butt went into the office and rang Sullivan and put his idea of David Jason for Del Boy.

Adding to David's astute portrayal of Del Boy was John Sullivan's wonderful way with words. Into David's mouth he planted such gems as 'dipstick', 'lovely jubbly' and 'cushty', not to mention the extraordinary phrase 'bonnet de douche' when raising a glass as a toast – words which gave Del a language almost of his own.

Sullivan claims that 'dipstick' was the only one he actually invented. The word 'plonker', he says, was used when he was a kid and 'lovely jubbly' was an advertising slogan for a triangular-shaped frozen orange drink which he suddenly remembered and decided to resurrect. Recently Sullivan was not a little astonished to find a hairdresser innocently using the words 'lovely jubbly' while tending his wife's hair.

The generic origins of 'cushty' purport to come from soldiers in India where there was apparently a place called Cushtabar which was supposed to be the

The rapport between David and Nick was one of the essential ingredients in the success of *Only Fools and Horses*.

easiest place if you ever got to it. Its nickname was Cushty. 'Bonnet de douche' evolved during filming of an *Only Fools and Horses* Christmas Special in the Kent seaside resort of Margate. Sullivan in fact stayed at a hotel in Ramsgate which regularly plays host to the French. In his hotel shower Sullivan found there was a shower cap with the words 'bonnet de douche' printed on it. With his keen eye for words, Sullivan seized on it and ended the evening toasting everyone with the words 'bonnet de douche' and subsequently wrote it into Del's vocabulary.

To complete Del Boy's portrait, Sullivan dreamed up the idea of giving Del a three-wheel Robin Reliant van in which to drive around. Sullivan considered Del's image of rings, coat and briefcase and reckoned he would be practical enough to drive something that could carry all his gear around in. And yet he wanted it to be something that was almost opposite to Del's image. A three-wheeled van seemed to fit the bill and the BBC chose a yellow one. Sullivan gave it the final twist by dreaming up the inscription on the side: New York – Paris – Peckham.

Another vital ingredient to the show's success was David's remarkable relationship with Nicholas Lyndhurst. They developed a sixth sense about what the other was going to do and from the outset it has been a harmonious pairing. So smooth was their working relationship that it came as a severe shock to producer, cast and crew when out on location one day in the back streets of Ealing an argument developed between the two men while they were lunching together in their camper van.

Their van was parked close to the 'butty wagon' which meant that the crew had to file past it as they queued for their lunch. They could hear every word as David and Nicholas first raised their voices at each other and then suddenly launched into a vicious argument. It became a full-blown slanging match and nervous glances were exchanged among the crew as they heard shouts coming from inside the van and sounds of a struggle. Judging by the din, the two stars were swapping blows and throwing each other against the camper's walls.

Ominously all went quiet and then the door of the van burst open and out stormed David hurling some well-chosen insults over his shoulder at Nicholas which were duly returned with equal venom. The crew watched open-mouthed as David slammed the camper van door behind him and strode off down the street muttering to himself in a fury.

The director and crew were aghast. A whole series and four months of filming stretched ahead of them and the two stars had fallen out on the very first day. Gradually David was coaxed back and filming continued but with David and Nicholas sniping away at each other and communicating with each other only through a production assistant.

The air of tension lasted through the afternoon until the tea-break when David and Nicholas happily announced that their violent row had been merely a wind-up. Everyone heaved a collective vast sigh of relief. David and Nicholas enjoyed their joke hugely. The camper van in which they had engineered their fake row was fitted with a tinted-glass window and they had been able to watch the dismay on the faces of the director and crew as they listened to the argument seemingly reaching a violent crescendo. In fact David and Nicholas were splitting their sides inside the van as they threw cutlery, boots, and shoes at the van walls to make it sound as though they were engaged in a big fight.

There is a mutual respect and working friendship between the two stars that embraces camaraderie off the set as well. During filming of the second series at Studland Bay, Nicholas Lyndhurst reached the age of 21 but, in his own modest way, he had not told too many people that it was his 21st birthday.

When the day arrived, nobody wished him a happy birthday, there were no cards from the cast and crew and certainly no presents. Secretly he hoped a cake might be produced at lunchtime but nothing was forthcoming. He was not too upset but merely thought that at least he could enjoy a few celebratory drinks with the film unit in the hotel bar at the end of the day.

On entering the bar, Nicholas was downcast to find it empty. The few crew members he saw wandering around the lobby declined his offer of a drink, announced they were off to Bournemouth for a meal and disappeared. Finally David came down from his room and a by-now desperate Nicholas blurted out that it was his birthday. David expressed surprise but immediately offered to buy Nicholas a drink in the bar.

Over a drink, David suggested playing a practical joke on Lennard Pearce. Why didn't they both go down to the gym that was being used as the wardrobe room and superglue Lennard Pearce's shoes to the floor? So off they went to the gym and as they walked in Nicholas was greeted by all the cast and crew, champagne, flags, banners and presents. Nicholas was so overcome he was close to tears.

Given that David and Nicholas worked so well together and quickly established a rapport, it was vital that Lennard Pearce should dovetail in as granddad. As it transpired, both David and Nick took an instant liking to Lennard and admired his acting ability.

If viewers had their way, *Only Fools and Horses* would have run for ever. It has proved consistently popular across the widest range of viewers from Hackney to Harrods, and Her Majesty the Queen is a particular fan. She particularly loves to watch the Christmas episodes which are inclined to include a few more laughs than her own seasonal broadcast.

Nicholas Lyndhurst also discovered that Prince Edward was a fan while working one day in the theatre at Windsor doing a Peter Shaffer play. On the last night Nicholas generously bought a couple of large bottles of whisky as a thank you to the crew and after the curtain call he flew back to the dressing room to collect them, tucked them under each arm and went back on stage. He was threading his way through a group of people on the stage when he felt a tap on the shoulder. It was Prince Edward with a request to Nicholas to appear in the Royal *It's a Knockout* programme.

'They had this wonderful chemistry. David was perfect all along and I didn't realise just how perfect he was for the part.'

The publicity-sensitive Lyndhurst happily accepts the price of fame because he enjoys playing the part so much. 'We both have such a fantastic laugh sometimes. I think David and I both agree that the chandelier episode – when the Trotters were engaged to clean the elegant old chandeliers in a country mansion – was one of our favourites.'

Above:
With Nicholas
Lyndhurst and
a friend.

Opposite Page:
David in 1996.

The episode was called 'A Touch of Glass' and John Sullivan rates it the hardest one he had to write. He said, 'I never write a script from page one onwards. I start somewhere in the middle or towards the end and I'll move backwards and forwards from that incident. "A Touch of Glass" was the hardest because I wrote it from the end when the chandelier falls because it was a true story that my dad told me. When he was an apprentice plumber they worked on this big house and it happened. He was telling me the saga to try to remind me to double check everything was all right and don't ever just trust your luck. I was laughing and the old man's telling me "Seven men lost their jobs through that." I told David this one day and he said, "Please, please. Do it!" So I went away and wrote the end. But I had to think how did they get there? What are the Trotters doing in this big house?' Perfectionist Sullivan said, 'I have always felt with that one that the beginning didn't really work that well.'

But Nicholas Lyndhurst remembers it for a different reason. 'Even the mock-up chandeliers that were made for us were very expensive and obviously we could only do the shot where we let it crash to the floor once, so we were ordered by producer Ray Butt to be on our very best behaviour.

'David and I both have a problem with giggling from time to time and just before filming started Ray took me to one side and gave me this really stern warning. He said, "If you laugh, you've not only blown the end of the episode you've wasted hundreds of thousands of pounds so not only are you off the set you're off the series." I was terrified. I thought, "He really means it."

'When we got up the ladders and started doing the final shots I was really determined to keep a straight face and after the chandelier fell Ray wanted to keep filming us looking astonished for a long time. That went on for what seemed like ages and I was struggling to hold it. Then just out of the corner of my eye I saw Ray watching and he quietly put his hand in his pocket, pulled out his handkerchief and put it in his mouth to stop himself laughing. Tears were running down his face. He had only been winding me up about the threat of the sack to make sure he got the shot. I did manage to see the joke later.'

Lennard Pearce's brilliance at creating Granddad's blissful ability to do the wrong thing from the best intentions was never better illustrated. What made the smashing finale even more funny was Granddad, totally oblivious to the disaster he had just caused by being in the wrong place at the right time, asking in all innocence: 'Alright Del Boy?'

Butt was not sure of Lennard's true age when he picked him for Granddad but in one of the early series he let slip that he had just got his bus pass. Butt also only later discovered that Lennard had been desperately ill for a long time and had thought his career was finished. In his maudlin moments Lennard would tell Butt that he had thought he would never work again and profusely thanked him. Lennard had thought at that stage he would not even be alive and yet there he was, suddenly a nationally known figure thanks to *Only Fools and Horses*.

The series never came closer to ending prematurely than when Lennard suddenly had a heart attack and died. It happened in the winter of 1984 and John Sullivan was the first to get the grim news. Lennard's landlady telephoned him to say that he had been taken to hospital in Hampstead.

Sullivan and actress Jan Francis, who was also a good friend of Lennard's, dropped everything and went to visit him. Sullivan took with him a little pig for good luck. In the *Only Fools and Horses* production box there had been a little pig called Trotter which had been lost and Sullivan took Lennard another one, Son-of-Trotter, and left it with Lennard at the hospital.

But a day later Lennard Pearce was dead and when John broke the news to David and Nick they were devastated. Off-screen there was a pecking order that David and Nicholas had continued half-heartedly to play and Lennard was like a real grandfather to them.

Lennard's death had occurred two weeks into filming an episode in which Granddad kept falling down the cellars and getting compensation. Lennard had shot his last scenes on a cold snowy Sunday morning outside Kingston Crown Court and was not due to film again till the following Sunday. But when word came through he had died, everyone was too shocked to continue and filming was immediately abandoned out of respect to Lennard.

David Jason said, 'It was a great shock. He was a wonderful actor and he had become a great friend. We were devastated. Lennard was so much a part of the show that I didn't know if we would be able to go on, or even want to. It's as if we have lost our real Granddad.'

After the funeral, David Jason, Nicholas Lyndhurst, Ray Butt and John Sullivan had a meeting with new BBC comedy chief Gareth Gwenlan to decide what to do. Christmas was approaching and eventually it was decided to pick up filming in the New Year. None of them could bear the thought of another actor taking on the role of Granddad and the only alternative was to introduce a new character. David said, 'He couldn't just be replaced. In the series we just couldn't have drafted in a lookalike so we decided that Granddad would die, just as Lennard had.

'We did what families do. We had a funeral. But the TV funeral was recorded not that long after we had been to the real funeral so it was very hard for all concerned.'

That immediately threw the burden on to John Sullivan who was finding Lennard's death very difficult to deal with. 'Writing a script without him was like trying to put my coat on with only one arm. It just didn't work any more.' But in spite of his feelings he quickly re-wrote the first two episodes to convey to viewers that Granddad had been taken into hospital although he was not seen. He also created a new character, Uncle Albert.

Butt now had the problem of casting the new hastily-written-in character of Uncle Albert but was astonished to find that news of Lennard's death had spread so quickly that within 48 hours he was inundated with letters from actors who wanted to replace him. Still desperately upset personally at Lennard's death, Butt slung them all on to a window sill and went away to Suffolk for Christmas resolving to look through them on his return from the festive break.

While he was away Butt came up with one or two possible replacements but the established actors he contacted were reluctant to step into Lennard's shoes. They knew that Lennard was going to be a hard act to follow – not just because he was such a good character but because he was so well liked by the public.

With filming due to pick up again on January 2, Butt drove back to London on New Year's Eve and went into the office determined to sort the problem out. He started sifting through the letters he had thrown on the windowsill and most quickly went into the bin. Then he came across a letter written in his own hand from a man with a beard called Buster Merryfield who included details of his life and mentioning that he was a retired bank manager and a late-comer to acting. That was certainly different.

Lennard was going to be a hard act to follow...

Butt picked up the phone and rang him at his home where Buster told him that he was currently in pantomime playing Baron Stoneybroke in Cinderella at Windsor. He was due on stage for a matinee at 2.30 pm but had time to go into the BBC to meet Butt and still make it to Windsor for his matinee performance.

At that point Butt had never heard of Uncle Albert and all he was able to do was ask Buster to read existing scripts for the character of Granddad. He was impressed and later rang David, Nicholas, and Sullivan to arrange a meeting at which Buster could read with them all. They duly came in and they all sat down in a dressing room in Television Centre and read together with Buster. They all agreed Buster was in and four days later he was costumed up on set ready for filming.

Buster himself could hardly believe it. For 40 years he had worked in a bank dreaming all the while of being an actor. At 57 he had taken retirement and within a week of leaving he was performing in repertory at the Connaught Theatre in Worthing. Then suddenly he had a key role in Britain's best-loved comedy show.

While Buster was being cast, Sullivan was hard at work on the re-writes. He felt that the Trotters were like a family to the viewers as well and therefore insisted on writing in Granddad's funeral. It had to be real, he felt, and seen to happen. He did not want suddenly to say that Granddad had gone off somewhere, or that he had taken a holiday, and for him never to be seen again. But Sullivan did not know how he was going to write an inevitably sad funeral of a much-loved character into a comedy show.

There was no way either that the series could open with Del and Rodney at the graveside. So, for only the second time, Sullivan wrote an episode without Granddad and tried to take the pain away by saying he was in hospital. Cleverly, Sullivan's re-writes also allowed newcomer Buster Merryfield to gain immediate sympathy from the viewers by having him get the gravestone for his departed brother.

Far and away Sullivan's hardest problem was how to write the actual funeral scene where Del and Rodney paid their great respects, where there was sorrow and grief, and yet he had to make it funny because it was a comedy show. Sullivan realised by the end of the scene he had to break away from the gloom and make the audience laugh with relief.

Brilliantly he came up with the idea of Granddad's old hat being buried with him but at the very end of the scene it turned out that it was the vicar's hat which had been buried by mistake.

For David and Nicholas, filming the funeral scene was hard to bear coming so soon after Lennard's real funeral. But somehow they got through it – and *Only Fools and Horses* lived on.

David Jason lent his weight to the campaign to extend the length of the episode. He said, 'We found that there were wonderful scenes that we had cut in the past that suddenly came back to life. I remember Uncle Albert's marvellous story about being lookout on a ship in the middle of the Atlantic during War and hitting an aircraft carrier that he somehow failed to notice. That had been taken out so many times because it never had anything to do with any storyline. It was just a wonderfully evocative slice of life that John is always so brilliant at creating.'

David likened playing Del Boy to wearing a comfy pair of old slippers. 'You know, when people say, "What are those terrible old slippers you've got on?" And you say: "I know, but they ain't half comfortable. They fit every contour."'

'We always knew there was still life in Only Fools.'

Del and Rodney did develop as the years went on. Del acquired a mobile phone, designer suits and by the late 80s even red braces. David said, 'He's now modelling himself on Gordon Gekko from the film *Wall Street*. He might not look like Michael Douglas but he reckons he's got the same style. It's fairly typical of Del to want to appear flashy. Every crooked little deal he makes is the one he thinks will make him a million, like a City slicker.'

John Sullivan had been reluctant to continue writing *Only Fools and Horses*, feeling that he should be moving on to fresh projects. But public demand and an appeal from the actors persuades him to switch his mind back to Peckham's Nelson Mandela House. David said, 'We talked him into writing one more Christmas special and one more series and I was thrilled to bits. We always knew there was still life in *Only Fools* but without the writer's willingness it could never live on.' Sullivan fed in the changes in his skilfully imperceptible

Opposite Page:
With Lesley Joseph, who plays Dorian in *Birds of a Feather*.

way as Rodney's relationship with Cassandra grew into a grown up thing. David said, 'Rodney's affair will be a lot more successful than Del's flirtation with the Yuppie world. Del could never really mix with the upper crusters.'

Rodney and Cassandra married in February 1989 in a brilliant landmark episode that reduced David Jason to genuine tears. 'It was a sad moment for Del and me – we cried real tears together. It was emotional because Nick and I have worked so closely together and I knew that Del realises for the first time that Rodders has grown up. It was a nostalgic moment, probably the most emotional in my life.'

Viewers were moved too as honeymoon-dazed Rodney finished his first day back at work and then returned to the grotty flat that he shared with Del and Uncle Albert. That gave Del the highly charged last words, 'You don't live here any more, you plonker!' The episode is a personal favourite of David's. He said, 'John Sullivan approached me and said he wanted to put some music in and asked me if I had heard the record 'You Keep Me Hanging On'. I'm not a great music person so he sent me the tape. He wanted to put it in at the moment Del was left alone. We constructed that moment very carefully to make it moving because we did not want to cheapen it.'

Del Boy has been able to move with the times.

The series is treated with enormously tender loving care by just about everyone concerned. At the start of the 1990s David Jason suggested Del's behaviour be improved a notch or two. He summed up his attitude. 'You won't be seeing Del smoke, drink or swear as much as he used to. On the show we all feel that we have a social responsibility, so we decided to cut things down.

'When we were filming the producer came up and said, "We have used the word bloody twice in one scene. Do we need it?" I said, "Yes" but I took the point. We are trying to have a collective responsibility. I might have the odd smoke but Del won't be swigging cocktails and puffing cigars like he used to.'

As the many millions of regular viewers noticed, at the finish of each series there was always a question mark over whether this might really be the end of *Only Fools and Horses*. It was partly because Sullivan cleverly wrote a neat conclusion which could provide a final curtain for the series if either David or Nicholas decided they no longer wanted to carry on. There was Rodney's wedding, Del's joyous moment of fatherhood, and another episode in which Del had the opportunity to go to Australia with Jumbo Mills.

Thanks to Sullivan's keen observation of people and life, Del Boy has been able to move with the times. Del's liking for a cocktail drink topped off with an umbrella owes its existence to a visit Sullivan made to a pub he had not been to for many years in London's Old Kent Road.

He noticed that nearby there were cocktail bars and dropped in to find that the tough guys with calluses on their knuckles who used to like a pint were now drinking umbrella-topped cocktails.

The most important shift of emphasis for David came after Sullivan had introduced Tessa Peake-Jones as Del's new girlfriend Raquel in a Christmas special. For much of the episode it appeared that Raquel was a resting actress until she was revealed, much to Del's humiliation, as a stripogram girl when she peeled off her police woman's uniform in front of Del and all his friends at his local.

Tessa's TV impact was immediate on her own life. When she went into her local pub shortly after the episode had been screened, they started playing 'Slow Boat to China' on the 60-year-old piano. And so much mail poured in about Raquel that Sullivan seized an opportunity to bring her back in an episode where Del and the lads are on a boy's outing to Margate. Sullivan listens to the fans and he knew he had done the right thing when he found people coming up to him in the newsagent's and the baker's thanking him for reviving Raquel.

It was no surprise when Tessa was given an expanded role in the next series. First she moved in with Del then became pregnant and provided Del with a son and heir.

David has always adhered to the theory that, in comedy shows in particular, if the cast all get on well together then it makes for a successful show. David and Tessa hit it off from the start. 'She's a super actress, super to work with,' he said, adding what a bonus that was for the series where Raquel moved into Del's home. 'If you're playing someone you are supposed to be in love with, you've got to be able to do things that are believable.'

One of the most difficult scenes David has ever had to play as Del Boy was when Tessa Peake-Jones as Raquel gave birth. 'It was a very hard thing for me to do because I've never had any experience with babies and I just didn't know whether I could make it work,' he admitted.

David was so anxious to play the part convincingly that he studied childbirth videos. He certainly got it right – a staggering 18.9 million viewers tuned in to watch Del become a dad.

The scene became a television triumph. David said, 'The videos were quite an eye opener. I have to say that Tessa was very securely dressed in that area. I think she had 14 pairs of knickers on. When I read the script I phoned John Sullivan up and told him he had out-Sullivaned Sullivan. It was the funniest, most moving, silliest, strangest, weirdest, oddest, warmest script ever. It was wonderful. I just fell about. I kept shutting the pages up and laughing and laughing. Then I couldn't wait to read the next page as I was already inventing what I was going to do. It was magical.

'It was the funniest, most moving, silliest, strangest, weirdest, oddest, warmest script ever.'

'I loved it after the baby was born and Del is a father. He has always had this thing about his mum and he takes the baby over to the window and looks out at the stars and gives a monologue about his son to his mother: "I'll give you what I never had 'cos I've always been a bit of a wally." Del says, "I have been a dreamer, son. You're going to have to live my dreams for me and do all the things I wanted to do. You're going to have to tell me all about them. Tell me if they were as good as I thought they would be." Here was this great wheeler-dealer who lays the birds really pouring his heart out in a very moving soliloquy. And it's all the more effective because Del is the sort of guy who thinks a soliloquy is a new sort of cocktail. John Sullivan knows just how to get right to an audience. He is marvellous because he is so dedicated. He worries and worries and spends hours and hours honing a script to perfection.

'You have to put credit where credit is certainly due. Without the ability of

great writers I would be nowhere. Since I have been in a position to have some control over work, I evaluate everything against John Sullivan's high standards. There are some wonderful writers in this country but I consider John Sullivan to be the best. Not only is that my opinion but it is a view shared by many writers themselves. John is very much a writer's writer. He also happens to be a lovely, genuine man which is a great bonus.

'One of the reasons I am able to keep going is that I try very hard to form teams of people to work together in which everyone gets on. I attempt not to have too much gossip, back-biting and unhappiness, I don't want that. It is very difficult to have a happy team. I like working with people who are fun, who are as committed to the programme as everyone else, and who take the mickey a lot. I don't go and shut myself away in the caravan. Most of the time I am out with the crew, behind the camera, wherever there is something interesting going on. Not only do I find it interesting but I also find it keeps people's spirits up.

'I could lock myself away in my caravan but I don't think that is very productive. I also think I can learn a lot. One day I would like to direct a television film. I would like to pass on my experience of comedy. I think *Only Fools* lasted so long because it's not a cardboard cutout show. It's very three dimensional. It has the range to swing from comedy to tragedy. It goes right across society now. It used to be considered rather common but everyone watches *Only Fools* now.'

David's enthusiasm for Del always springs from the scripts. 'I never tire of reading John Sullivan's writing. Sometimes it's only minutes after they have come through the letterbox that I've collapsed with laughing. I loved the moment when Buster Merryfield as Uncle Albert was telling one of his interminable Navy stories and he admitted he was on lookout when they crashed into another very large ship. Del says, "You mean that you were on watch and you actually ran into a 45,000 ton aircraft carrier. Blimey, they'd have been better off with Ray Charles in the crow's nest." '

'It has the range to switch from comedy to tragedy.'

Albert's abilities as a lookout are a frequent source of mirth. At the start of the fabulous Jolly Boys' Outing to Margate Albert fails to warn Del, working like mad to sell some dodgy car radios, of the approach of the law. Del flips. 'The entire massed band of the Metropolitan Police Force could march past singing "I Shot The Sheriff" without him noticing them.'

For Christmas 1991 the BBC really splashed out and flew Del and Rodney and the rest of the crew to Miami for a two-part adventure that was a real departure from life in drizzly Peckham. Locals were baffled by the anxiety of BBC security staff holding blankets to prevent photographers recording these two totally unknown actors at work. They headed for Florida when Rodney won a competition but ended up on the run from the Mafia as Del turned out to be the double of a deadly mobster. Sadly as soon as they arrived in the sunshine state more than 15 inches of rain fell delaying filming by five days. 'We might as well have been in Margate,' said David. 'The weather was absolutely awful. It should have been stable and sunny, but it rained furiously for the first week and we found ourselves in deep water. We have had to have 5 am starts ever since to catch up. But it was a high class production and it was enormous fun. Mind you, the Americans in the crew kept getting confused about the script. We had to keep stopping to explain to them what a "git" was and what "lovely jubbly" meant.'

Producer Gareth Gwenlan had to deal with the complex American labour regulations and did not enjoy the process. 'We had terrible trouble with the US unions,' he said. 'But the real Mafia were fine. I would say that it wasn't that successful but Jason's performance was wonderful.'

Former BBC head of comedy Gwenlan took over after Ray Butt left the BBC. Always ultra professional he did everything he could to maintain the high standards of the show. And was not afraid to speak up when levels dropped. He felt "A Royal Flush", the 1986 Christmas special about the Trotters on a country weekend, was not up to scratch. 'I wanted to cut out 20 minutes. Oh God, it went on and on. It was made under the most difficult of circumstances ever. John had great difficulty writing it. It was filmed in the middle of December under the most awful weather. We only had daylight for four hours. David and Nick were both ill with 'flu. The tent scene was filmed in the middle of the night with lights to make it look like daylight. The fact that it was ever shown was a miracle, but my favourite moment is seeing Del with the pump action shotgun.'

One of the big disappointments of Gwenlan and the rest of the team is that *Only Fools* humour is so essentially British that it does not sell overseas. Gwenlan said, 'It doesn't sell anywhere. We've tried to sell to Australia like *Minder* which is one of the biggest sellers. It did sell a little to Scandinavia.

America would never like it as it's based on an ethos that they find odd. They don't like losers.

'But if it were up to the top brass of the BBC it would be on twice a week like a soap opera. A week does not go by when I don't get a phone call from the controller saying, "Is there going to be one this year or any chance of a series?"'

In March 1991 David Jason finally won a British Oscar at the sixth attempt. After repeatedly losing out to more fashionable stars like Rowan Atkinson and Victoria Wood for the light entertainment gong, the *Only Fools and Horses* star was delighted and made a pledge which delighted fans of the series. He had previously taken the BAFTA best actor award for his dramatic role in *Porterhouse Blue* but he was delighted to gatecrash the comedy clique. He said, 'We have been making the series for 10 years and there is no reason why it can't go on for another 10 years.' With typical generosity he singled out John Sullivan for special mention saying simply, 'He gives me the ammunition and I fire the guns.'

Yet there was an edge of frustration in the background. The relationship between the BBC and David Jason and the rest of the show was often never quite as harmonious behind the scenes as it looked on the surface and the 10 year reference was a heavy public hint to the people in power at the BBC. David said frankly, 'No one has told me that we will be carrying on. I wish they would. There has been talk of another Christmas special and I have discussed storylines but there has been a deafening silence from the BBC. It puts me in an embarrassing position. Del is my top priority but I do have lots of other offers of work and I need to know where I stand.'

But it only comes over as so effortlessly funny because everyone involved with the show works incredibly hard. One of the most memorable moments over the 16 years of *Only Fools and Horses* was the time Del, by now a would-be Yuppie, was on the chat-up in a wine bar and ended up falling flat when he leaned on a bar flap not noticing it had been lifted. Instead he found himself leaning on air.

In March 1991 David Jason finally won a British Oscar.

John Sullivan wrote the classic pratt-fall into the script of the 'Yuppy Love' episode after seeing a flash Harry missing his footing one night when he went to lean on a bar. Sullivan recalls, 'The scene was not in the original script because we couldn't get Roger Lloyd-Pack for Trigger. I got a last minute phone call saying they could get Roger for one day, did I want to do anything? We had them in the wine bar and we had a bit of time because the script was a bit short and I thought I'd bring in the scene I'd seen in a wine bar in Balham. It's become a sort of classic scene but it was written in ten minutes.'

It looked an easy scene for David to do. But the natural instinct of anyone falling is to try to break the fall. David turned it into one of TV's unforgettably funny moments by falling down like a log. It is one of the most memorable *Only Fools* moments but for David Jason it was another exercise in faultless comedy technique. He recalls, 'When John told me about the Flash Harry missing his footing he said that the guy had recovered himself just in time and then looked round the room to make sure nobody had seen his mistake. He did not see John looking and was delighted no one had seen him.

'I said, "It's brilliant, John. But I would have to do the whole fall." He replied,

"No, that's not the way I saw it." I said, "I know that's not the way you saw it but if I do it I want to do the whole fall." He said, "OK, I'll put it in."'

What became a magical moment for millions of viewers was really the result of meticulous planning. David Jason took John Sullivan's amusing idea and went to work. 'First of all we had to have a shot of Del Boy and Trigger with the flap going up and going down while they have their conversation. Then you had to drag the viewers' attention away over to the two girls and then have a shot of Del leaning against the bar. Then Del says, "Just act casual, Trig," as the barman comes out and leaves the flap up and we cut across to the two girls again to distract the viewers. Then we come back to Del falling.'

The result was one of the funniest moments in the show's long and happy history. But for David it was, 'A good idea, a lot of work, and a lot of construction. It's a bit of science, it's a bit of experience and it's a bit of knowledge, but you have to work at it. I had a very small mattress to fall onto. And that is the bit that is extremely difficult. It is the difference between being real and comic. The problem is when you fall you go so far and then your instincts take over and your head and eyes will turn to see. Then your arm goes out, then your leg. The difficult part is not obeying your instincts and going against what is natural. It's funnier that way. Also while I was down I got somebody to give me a wine glass so that when I got up I still looked as though I had the same full wine glass. How many people noticed that I don't know. It was just another funny little joke that we put in. Just the other day a chap came up to me and said, "You know when you fell through the bar?" I said, "Yeeees." He said, "Tell me something because I've got money on this. Did you rehearse it or was it an accident?" How's that for professionalism! That's how high my abilities are regarded! In some ways I suppose that was a backhanded compliment. The guy meant it. People think that if it's comedy, it's only daft, whereas a great heavy piece of drama is seen as desperately artistic.'

The idea that *Only Fools* is guilty of glamorising petty crime is firmly rejected by David Jason. 'We do have a responsibility. We know we do. There is always a danger of being imitated by stupid people. If we were shown jumping off the Clifton Suspension Bridge I dare say some wally would try to emulate it. We always show that Del is essentially a failure. And when it comes to the crunch he is actually very honest. He is also very vulnerable. If he was harder and more successful there would be more danger of him glamorising cheap thiefdom.'

Over the years, the *Only Fools and Horses* cast and production teams have watched the show grow in popularity to the point now where Christmas is not Christmas unless TV viewers can sit back and watch the Trotter family in a TV special. Every year it was the jewel in the BBC's festive TV crown. But Christmas 1996 with the three-show series amazingly capped everything that had gone before.

With David Jason and Nicholas Lyndhurst both in great demand for other projects it took 14 months planning just to get them together to film the ground-breaking three-parter. The story had Del and Rodney discovering they had an incredibly rare Harrison watch in an old lock-up. And with typical Sullivan brilliance Rodney recalled from a scene in the very first episode, 16 years earlier, exactly where the receipt was. It was as though *Only Fools* had gone full

With Gillian Hinchcliffe, the woman who has brought love back into David's life.

circle. The shows were simply packed with magical moments but the sight of Del and Rodney dressed as Batman and Robin still lives in most people's memories as one of the funniest sight of all time. The audiences were sensational: 21.31 million, 21.33 million and 24.35 million for the fabulous finale which had Del, Rodney and Uncle Albert wandering up the Yellow Brick Road with their £6 million fortune. There wasn't a dry eye in millions of houses when that went out on December 29.

And although it was officially intended to be the end the success and the joy of the reunion shows had all concerned considering another *Only Fools and Horses* possibly around the time of the Millennium. Sadly the death of Buster Merryfield in 1999 finally put paid to the idea of yet another revival. David Jason, Nicholas Lyndhurst and John Sullivan all agreed that *Only Fools and Horses* simply would not be the same without Buster.

Only Fools and Horses has millions of faithful followers but none more devoted that the band who have formed themselves into the official Only Fools and Horses Appreciation Society. Perry Aghajanoff and Andy Banks run the club from their homes in Essex. They put out a lively quarterly magazine called

Hookie Street and enjoy good relationships with the cast and the BBC. Membership is growing fast and *Only Fools* followers from as far afield as Croatia and Bangkok have joined up.

But confirmed workaholic David Jason is never one to rest on his laurels. And when Yorkshire TV asked him to consider new projects they came up with yet another hit. David recalled, 'It took me completely by surprise. It was the first time anything like that had ever happened to me. We talked about various ideas and I explained I'd always liked detective series. I watch the *Starsky and Hutch* and *Cagney and Lacey* type of series but for me they have never been as interesting as *Inspector Morse*, the *Wexford* series, and *Taggart* and *Columbo*. I like the sort of detective who unravels the mystery, not the ones who go around blowing people away.

'As soon as I'd read it I said, " That's the one. Get me Frost."'

'During the lunch I said that I felt there was an area which British TV had been missing out on – a copper who was a bit off-the-wall, a bit odd, a down-to-earth detective a man who is overworked but has a sense of humour, a man who has a sense of sympathy for the victims for a change and isn't just out to beat up the crook. So Yorkshire TV said: right, leave it to us.

'*Frost* was just one of three books Yorkshire came up with and as soon as I'd read it I said: "That's the one. Get me Frost!" I knew it would be a tremendous challenge but one of the reasons I wanted the challenge of taking on a major dramatic role like Frost was that it had never been offered to me before.'

When David signed to play Detective Inspector Jack Frost in a brand new police drama series for Yorkshire TV, it still represented something of a risk. His acting credentials were deeply rooted in comedy. Yorkshire TV supremo Vernon Lawrence was sure David would comfortably manage the sharp change in direction which the role of Frost clearly required. In the first episodes, Frost would be a detective investigating such crimes as multiple murders, violent armed robbery and the poisoning of a football star – a stark contrast with Del Boy's petty schemes and scams and Pop Larkin's golden-hearted what's-mine-is-yours way of life.

After the first two-hour film had been shown to a private audience David was jubilant. 'Some people said they thought I could never do this sort of thing,' he said. 'But those who have seen *Frost* confessed that they forgot about me after the first few minutes and they got drawn into the story.'

That two-hour opening film of *A Touch of Frost* was screened on December 6, 1992 and pulled in the incredible audience of nearly 18 million, an audience share of 73% of people watching TV at the time. It was way beyond Yorkshire TV's expectations and the first series reached an average audience of 16 million.

David says, 'Sometimes the police are painted badly on television and I hope Frost redresses the balance the other way to a degree. He's a rather old-fashioned policeman, a policeman like we want them all to be. He's honest, he cares, he has no time for the criminal but believes the victim should be cared for. I enjoy playing Frost, not least because he's got a lovely sense of humour and that's fun to get across. You'd imagine with his lonely personal life he'd be a bit depressing. But not a bit. There are lots of facets to him. I admire him because he's opinionated and because he's totally dedicated which is one of the reasons he's lonely at times.'

David also chose to set a personal example about cigarette smoking in *A Touch of Frost*. 'Frost is a chain-smoker in the books and that was very much part of his character,' he says. 'But I felt we should be socially aware and mindful that a lot of people were trying to give it up. So I told Yorkshire TV I wasn't going to chain-smoke on screen. For a start I'd fall over dead – although I do smoke a bit, maybe a few cigarettes in the evening but none during the day. What I asked was: do we need this socially? It's not a good idea any more to smoke. So we hit on the idea of making Frost a smoker who is giving up the habit. That way, the idea was there all the time but I didn't actually chain-smoke.

'I had to smoke a couple of cigarettes but mainly I was lighting up and being told to stub it out. I feel I must set an example. It's the same with swearing on TV. I always ask: do we need it? I want more people to watch me, not less. That means families watching and I believe you can be real on TV without resorting to language of the gutter. I don't like going past a bus stop and hearing loads of kids aged seven or eight effing and blinding.

'When I was a kid I used to get a whack if I said the word "bloody". And if we were standing at a bus stop being a bit rowdy we'd get a clip round the ear from a man who'd say: "Cut that out, there's ladies present." We might have pulled a face behind the man's back but we certainly shut up.

'So if I don't like swearing, why should I encourage people to do it? I feel the question as far as TV goes should be "Can we avoid it? Do we need it?" People may say, "Ah yes, but people swear in real life". Yes they do. But do you like it?'

Rejecting the sex and violence which has often been so fashionable in TV cop shows, *A Touch of Frost* captured that crucial audience of both men and women and prospered beyond everyone's hopes at Yorkshire TV.

David and his brother Arthur shared some excellent comic scenes in the last series of *A Touch of Frost*. Arthur played quirky collator Ernie Trigg, the copper in charge of the station files and the source on endless meticulously ordered information who became one of Jack Frost's closer confidants. The brothers worked wonderfully well together and it gave Arthur the chance to move, for a moment, out of the shadow of his more famous younger brother. Arthur said, 'In the early days people would say to Dave, "Aren't you Arthur White's brother?" Now it's the other way round of course. '

David and his brother Arthur shared some excellent comic scenes in the last series of *A Touch of Frost*.

On March 2, 1997, ITV screened a highly emotional edition *A Touch of Frost*. David had millions of viewers dewy-eyed as he shed genuine tears on screen as Frost grieved over the death of a woman friend. The scene was all the more moving because the nation knew he was drawing on the harrowing personal experience of watching his beloved Myfanwy Talog's own decline towards death. 'It was an incredibly difficult scene to do,' said David, 'the hardest I've ever done.'

In the very first series of *A Touch of Frost*, Frost's screen wife had died of cancer. The parallels in David's own life were apparent for all to see. 18 months after Myfanwy had died, though, there was a new woman in his life. She was beautiful former Yorkshire TV assistant producer Gill Hinchcliffe who first emerged at David's side, happily basking in his reflected glory, at London's Royal Albert Hall where David received a standing ovation as he accepted a Special Recognition award at the National Television Awards presentation.

Gill met David when he was making *A Bit of A Do* and they had subsequently worked together on *A Touch of Frost*. Gradually they became close and the attractive 37-year-old blonde looked radiantly happy arm-in-arm with David at the star-studded party after the awards. Even the Spice Girls were momentarily ignored by photographers as they jostled each other for pictures of David Jason with the new woman in his life who, it was noted, bore some resemblance to Myfanwy with her sparkling eyes, ready smile and cropped hair.

'They are meant for each other. They make a wonderful pair and they are very much in love.'

Taking Gill to the awards was a very public statement by David that he had found love again and that he now did not care who knew it. Nor, it seemed, did Gill's mother. 'They are meant for each other. They make a wonderful pair and they are very much in love,' said Mrs. Hinchcliffe at her home at Mirfield, near Dewsbury, West Yorkshire.

Gill was understanding and she was also a soft shoulder for him to rely on. But it was not until David and Gill flew out to the Montreux TV festival as guests of the BBC in the spring of 1997 that he was able to reveal the extent of Gill's influence in his life. 'She's great,' he said. 'People are always asking me to do things all the time and I find it hard to relax. But she shields me from all of that pressure. She takes all my phone calls and keeps me relaxed so that I have to do the minimum of work. It's so nice to have someone as lovely as her who is so caring and loving, especially after what I've been through.'

The sociable fun of David's early years are a complete contrast to his life now. He lives in splendid isolation in his mansion, with Tony Blair as his new neighbour and Special Branch as his local neighbourhood watch. And it's only at home that he feels really happy. He is very, very careful about who he lets into his domain. Ronnie Barker, John Sullivan, Nicholas Lyndhurst and other trusted friends from the business come to dinner. But the house was bought really for Myfanwy. It's a fabulous place with a lake, a swimming pool and he has a tractor and acres of land. She loved the space and the scope it provided for her flair for decoration. But after she died David found it very difficult to be there on his own. Memories of Myfanwy were in every room and David threw himself into work to try to put some time and space between him and his tragedy. Now his relationship with caring Gill has blossomed friends say somehow the great house feels happy again.

But David's favourite times are not when hosting glittering dinner parties. Instead he much prefers the moments spent tinkering in his garage with something mechanical like one of his beloved motorbikes. One of the keys to the success of his love for Gill is that she loves to see him absorbed in his work. He is much more of a practical man than ever he is a thinker. And she sits for hours watching him with spanner or screwdriver in hand dismantling some old engine, his mind relaxed and blissfully happy to be in a world where there are no autograph hunters yelling, 'Oi you plonker!' Gill will even help and scrub all the carbon off a corroded part. They love gardening together and doing anything practical. He is not an intellectual, he's a man who prefers to do things with his hands rather than his brain. He loves to switch off and forget the ceaseless pressure of being Britain's number one television star and staying in that spot. At the end of the day he is a jobbing artisan, it's just that instead of making a few quid a day as an electrician he makes a few thousand as an actor. But he is haunted by the fear that it might all dry up.

Much of his insecurity is rooted in the knowledge that he is not really quite sure why he is so immensely popular and successful. He knows he can act most thespians off the screen but there is also an undefinable X factor which makes the public switch on to whatever he does on television.

Certainly it is not money that drives Jason. Several times in his career he has turned his back on the most lucrative options. And a senior TV executive who has negotiated with David on a string of projects insists he is a joy to deal with. 'He is probably only about number five in the league of top British actor earners behind Thaw and Cole and Waterman and Bolam. But he is number one in terms of audience attraction. If I had a script that I wanted to turn into a successful drama or comedy then I'd go for David first, second and third.' By the people in charge of British television David is rated as a second Chaplin, a comic genius who delivers fabulous performances and enormous audiences every time.

He is not really quite sure why he is so immensely popular and successful.

As he approaches his landmark 60th birthday in February 2000, David Jason remains as busy and in demand as ever. As well as working on a new series of *A Touch of Frost* he starred in the BBC's prestigious First World War film *All The King's Men*. Jason gave a stirring performance as the remarkable Royal employee Frank Beck who insisted, despite his age, on fighting alongside his much younger butlers, footmen and other workers in the 110-strong Sandringham Company of the Norfolk Regiment. The King ordered him to stay at home but he refused and perished after charging Turkish positions in 1915 at Gallipoli along with most of his men.

David Jason also set off to the Pacific to film another of his popular programmes about diving. He was heading for Pearl Harbour in Hawaii where wrecks still lie from the surprise Japanese attack on the US fleet in 1941. He shrugs off considerations of age and insists on living life to the full. 'My work is part of my life and I love my life,' he says with a grin. Britain's best-loved star certainly has no thoughts of taking life easy.

Postscript

David Jason's enormous army of armchair fans can breathe a giant collective sigh of relief. It appears that Britain's favourite funny man is at long last beginning to share the joke.

As the greatest comic actor in the land approaches his 60th birthday, friends and family have noticed a gradual, yet distinct, change in the dedicated individual they know and love. Much to their delight a new ease and sense of peace has developed deep within David Jason to replace his former rather anxious and driven attitude to his life and his craft.

Time has done much to soften the profound sense of loss caused by the deaths of his mother and his beloved long-term partner Myfanwy Talog. And his beautiful new lover Gill Hinchcliffe has helped David to start enjoying his richly deserved success and to convince him he no longer has anything to prove to his public. They love him just the way he is.

Life at the stylish mansion deep in the Buckinghamshire countryside has taken on a lighter, more open, atmosphere. The couple often entertain friends in the elegant house with sweeping grounds which border the neighbouring estate of Chequers, country home of the Prime Minister.

David and Gill have redecorated in brighter, younger colours and the house is now much more of a home and so much less of a refuge. David is enjoying life as never before, and although he still chooses to work hard it is more out of positive choice than the pressures of the old insecurities. A friend who visited recently said: 'David seems to have the sort of peace of mind he has never had before. He still rushes round keeping the gardens looking immaculate and he still potters about with the machines in his garage. But now he does it with a smile on his face and a spring in his step. Gill is very good for him certainly, but it's more than that. It's as if he has finally realised he has arrived and that his place in the public's affection is safe.'

Del was so astonished he fainted.

In 1999 he returned from a two-year break to play crumpled Inspector Jack Frost again saying: 'I needed a rest from being a policeman for a while because

111

I was spending my year being more of a policeman than I was an actor. So it was good for me to have a break and I think it was good for everybody. We've all come back with renewed energy.' More significantly he added: 'The death of Frost's wife made the character quite dark. But since that has drifted more and more into the past he has become much more amusing.'

David was deeply saddened by the death of his friend and *Only Fools and Horses* co-star Buster Merryfield which certainly put paid to any last hope of reviving Britain's best situation comedy. David and the third star Nicholas Lyndhurst certainly agree now it is best for the show to be remembered for the fabulous three final fortune-winning editions of Christmas 1996, particularly as the endlessly repeated show is now so well known to its faithful fans it would be almost impossible to top everything they have already done.

'He could read out the London telephone directory and get an audience.'

David prefers to look ahead and was rightly proud of the deeply moving BBC film *All The King's Men* in which he played real-life hero Captain Frank Beck. And with a new series of deep sea diving adventures filmed in the Pacific he has more than enough work to keep him busy.

But these days, for perhaps the first time in his life, David Jason is not completely driven by his work. Long experience of taking it all too much to heart has taught him to switch off and enjoy his home, his friends and his many exotic holidays with lover Gill. The scripts still arrive in their scores but these days they take a little longer to get read. David Jason will be 60 in February 2000 and he intends to enjoy many more happy birthdays after that one.